FINLAND

Gladys Nicol

FINLAND

B. T. Batsford, Ltd
London and Sydney

First pubished 1975
Copyright © Gladys Nicol, 1975

ISBN 0 7134 2995 x

Printed in Great Britain by
Richard Clay (The Chaucer Press) Ltd, Bungay, Suffolk
for the publishers,
B. T. Batsford Ltd, 4 Fitzhardinge Street, London W1H 0AH
and 23 Cross Street, Brookvale, NSW 2100, Australia

Contents

Illustrations

Acknowledgements

There are so many people, in Finland and in England, who have helped consciously or unconsciously with this book that it would require a small directory to list them. But special thanks are due to the following: *In Finland*: Hans and Brita Bolten, Urpo Hyry and Ann-Marie Pihlstrom, all of the Finnish Tourist Board, for their active help and constant encouragement; *In England*: Kari Jokilehto and Eero Alasvuo of the Finnish Tourist Board and Boris Taimitarha of Finnair for their practical assistance and endless patience; *In England and in Finland*: Phyllis Chapman, of the Finnish Tourist Board, who thought I ought to visit Finland in the first place. Most of all, my family for their understanding.

The Finnish Tourist Board's permission to reproduce photographs 7 and 16 is gratefully acknowledged; numbers 1–3, 5–6, 8, 11, 15, 19 and 20 are by A. F. Kersting; 4 and 13 are by René Longeval, the rest are by the author. The map was drawn by Patrick Leeson.

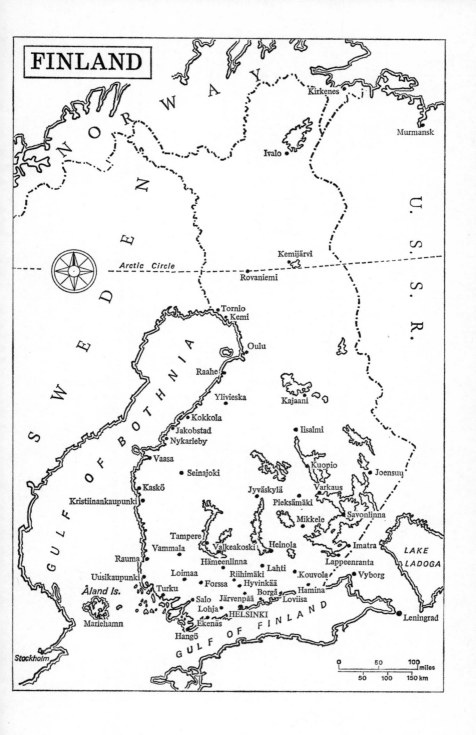

FINLAND

NORWAY

SWEDEN

U. S. S. R.

Kirkenes

Murmansk

Ivalo

Arctic Circle

Kemijärvi

Rovaniemi

Tornio
Kemi

Oulu

GULF OF BOTHNIA

Raahe

Ylivieska

Kajaani

Kokkola
Jakobstad
Nykarleby

Iisalmi

Vaasa

Seinäjoki

Kuopio
Varkaus
Joensuu

Kaskö

Jyväskylä

Kristiinankaupunki

Pieksämäki

Savonlinna

Mikkele

Tampere

Vammala
Valkeakoski
Heinola

Imatra

LAKE
LADOGA

Rauma

Hämeenlinna
Lahti
Lappeenranta

Loimaa
Riihimäki
Kouvola
Vyborg

Uusikaupunki
Forssa
Hyvinkää

Åland Is.
Turku
Borgå
Hamina

Salo
Järvenpää
Loviisa

Lohja
HELSINKI

Mariehamn
Ekenäs

Leningrad

Hangö

GULF OF FINLAND

Stockholm

0		50		100	
miles

50   100   150 km

For Fiona

1. Introducing Finland

It was quite a few years ago when, on a very hot day in June, I climbed to the lookout platform on the Olympic tower in Helsinki. Below lay modern houses, old apartments and the rambling streets of the city with its traffic and its trams. Some way behind me the sparkling waters of the Baltic shimmered in the heat haze, while ahead, the dark green pine- and fir-clad landscape, interspersed with the winking blue of lakes and rivers, melted into infinity on the horizon. 'There,' said Heikki, 'you have Finland.' It was true enough in a geographical sense. Finland is composed mainly of forests, lakes and rivers, with a heavy sprinkling of ultra-modern architecture, small wooden houses and a long and very beautiful coastline. But that is only the Finland one sees in a cursory glance, viewed from an isolated position on the top of a high vantage point. Indeed, if one only looks for the scenic qualities, there are vast areas where its very peacefulness and similarity might become monotonous, because this of all lands cannot be put into the 'If it's Tuesday, it must be Finland' class. It needs time and patience, for it does not put itself on show to everyone. It is not spectacular, except in parts of Lapland and in what is left of Karelia. Its beauty lies in its tranquillity, in its loneliness, and in the small, almost forgotten cameos of Nature—the movement of wind across water, the plop of a fish in the evening light, a bonfire on a summer beach, the white and violet silence of winter snows, the golden bronze of *ruska*, the Finnish autumn . . .

It is a little strange that this should be so, for Finland has been anything but peaceful in her long existence. This same gentle landscape has been the scene of some of the bloodiest battles and the peoples who have lived there have been subjected to violences and hardships of a sort that only man stoops to inflict on brother man. It is this background of constant struggle for survival which forms the basis of today's Finland: the platform upon which the Finnish nation has formed its character, for the people are indivisible from the land when one makes any sort of pronouncement on this, the least known of all the Scandinavian family.

I read once (and I cannot remember where it was so I cannot give a credit for it!) that while Norway, Sweden and Denmark are brothers, Finland is a well loved cousin. I think this is accurate, but I would go further and say that it is a family who live more or less in the same street but that the cousin is a product of a marriage between a member of the family and a stranger from afar. We cannot always choose our neighbours in the streets where we live. Neither can these people. The neighbours to the east of the cousins' house are rather of a tougher, rougher disposition than the neighbours to the west of the family holdings, so that the cousins, not unnaturally, prefer not to be in conflict with them if it is avoidable. It is not a case of 'Peace at any price', but rather 'Live, and let live' . . .

Let us look for a minute at the map. Finland is situated between the 60th and 70th degrees of latitude. Her boundary to the west, both on land and across the Gulf of Bothnia, is with Sweden, in the north, with Norway's Lapland, along the east with the Soviet Union, and in the south, across the Gulf of Finland, with Estonia, now swallowed by u.s.s.r. The whole country is a little bigger than the United Kingdom and Eire put together, being just over seven hundred miles in length and three hundred and thirty miles in width. (The official figures are precisely 721 and 336, but I have an aversion to statistics, because they bring so much that is vitally alive down to the bare bones of black figures on a white page.) The climate varies considerably, with long, damp, cold, often fierce winters, and surprisingly warm summers, particularly in Central Finland. Like elsewhere, the pattern of the weather has changed slightly, for in the past two winters there has been comparatively little snow in the Helsinki area, much to the disgust of the skiers, although the icebreakers around the coasts haven't been out of work. Of course, in the north and east the snow comes early and stays late. Lake Saimaa for instance is seldom icefree until May, while in Lapland, the *tunturi* (hills) keep pockets of snow on their shaded sides throughout the year and the best holiday skiing season is in April. The inland lakes are very warm in summer, thanks to the fact that they are comparatively shallow, following the contours of the countryside around them. Summer sea temperatures too can be surprising. Around the inner islands of the archipelago, the water can be as warm as off Northern Spain, although further out it assumes the chillier mien of say, Holland, Northern Germany or Kent.

The population of Finland today is coming up towards the five million mark, thanks to a general increase in longevity in the human race and, most important, the absence of war for the past three decades. They are a mixed lot. Among my own friends and acquaintances, both men and women, there are little fair ones, tall dark ones, short sturdy ones, big sturdy ones . . . Statistics (again) tell us that 86 per cent of Finnish men have blue or grey eyes and 82 per cent of the women have fair or light brown hair. This is probably very true, but I'm not sure that I would divide it quite like that. I find that the thing that most Finns have in common is the shape and expression around the eyes. Rather high cheekbones, with, on occasion, an almost inscrutable Eastern look which dissolves quickly when there is some instance of their dry, often Puckish humour. On the whole I find them a tenacious, rather reserved, obstinate, serious people, with intense emotions, but with a quick infectious wit and an ability to enjoy themselves when the opportunity arises. There seem to be no half measures in anything that they do. They either like or dislike—and show it. Perhaps this is why I like them so much. But there is a great respect for the guests within their borders. No-one could find better, or more generous hosts, but I think I am inclined to use an expression long used in my family . . . I would prefer to drink than to quarrel with them; they would make implacable enemies when roused. One look at their history confirms this. There is one rather overworked word which is used about the Finnish people—*Sisu*—much beloved by non-Finnish speakers who would like to think they have learned a little. It has many meanings, but mostly it means perseverance and pluck. Often the Finns have both. They sometimes say themselves that they are not quite sure whether they are trying to live up to the word, or whether the word is trying to live up to them. Perhaps it is a little of both . . .

These qualities however, are the universal ones. There are many differences in people who come from various parts of Finland. Those from Karelia for instance are shorter and heavier in build, betraying their closer links with Eastern Europe, and they tend to be more exotic in facial structure, flatter and broader of feature. They are livelier, using their hands in an extravagance of gesture more expected from the Latin, unlike their brethren from the West Coast who have an economy of words and movement unless prompted by liberal dosage of *kosken-korva*. People from Lapland (apart from the Lapps themselves who are a separate race), are even more sparing in expression. Yet with all the Finns I have met everywhere there is a responding friendliness which is heartwarming. They will always help, although in the polite manners of the Northern countries they sometimes hesitate to intrude unless one wishes it. In conversation there is often a pause before the reply comes, as though weighing everything said, and one cannot entirely put this down to finding the phrase in English or Swedish. They assess, and, as I am able to judge, having assessed, there is no deviation from the decision. Others might call that stubbornness, I prefer to name it reliability.

Among Finns who have lived away from the old country for some years I have heard criticism that Finns tend to be petty, nursing old grievances and grudging advancement. These are not faults confined to Finland. I have heard similar criticism from Finland-domiciled people, so perhaps there may be some justification, but I have never lived in Finland and am not qualified to judge.

But there is one facet of Finnish life which worries me, and that is the weakness for heavy drinking that is all too obvious sometimes. Many within Finland are worried too, and not only among the older generation. A young university girl told me that most of the young men she knew had nothing to do except drink *Pontikka*—that is, the outlawed dynamite, made in illicit stills, which passes for drink. This usually passes 'when they get a steady and reliable girl-friend'. Perhaps that again comes from the fact that there is little to do in long dark winters and in summer one drinks for the joy of it. I would like to think that someone could find a solution.

No-one seems to know for certain where the Finns come from. Even the origins of the tongue they speak are surrounded by obscurity. It belongs to a group called Finno-Ugrian, spoken by less than twenty million people, among them, Estonians, Hungarians and Finns. But the assumption that Finnish today is like Hungarian is wrong. I was talking to a Hungarian hairdresser who works with a Finnish colleague and they tried in vain to find common denominators in their speech, finally reverting to English. However, the professors probably know better. The Estonians and Finns have some similarity, so the presumption that the Finns found their way from Eastern Europe is probably correct. But over the years these two languages have diversified to the extent that although they use similar words the meanings can be quite different. I was listening one evening to a radio programme from Tallinn at the time of President Nixon's sortie into the u.s.s.r. and I asked a friend for a translation of the news bulletin. 'God knows,' he said. 'All I understood was "President Nixon and u.s.a . . . " '

Finnish is difficult to learn partly because of its grammar, but also because it is so dissimilar to European tongues. When learning Norwegian or Swedish, English, or preferably Scots, and German are both helpful. But Finnish . . . who on earth associates '*Kyllä*' with 'Yes'? To my ears, Finnish is pretty to listen to even without understanding it, and now I find it interesting to pick out differences between country dialects, still without much comprehension. In Savo for instance, sounds are flatter than in Helsinki, and in Karelia many of the words sound like Russian. They do in fact derive from that tongue in some cases. For someone intent on learning Finnish, it has one great advantage. It is pronounced exactly as it is written, but you must remember that emphasis is always on the first syllable. In my struggles to master words, I was told, with a twinkle in the eye of the speaker, 'In Finland we have plenty of time so we pronounce every syllable!' Finns are always delighted when one tries to learn even a word or two, so during one hilarious evening after sauna, friends decided that the most valuable word that I could possibly be taught would be '*Saippuakauppias*' . . . because (they maintained), it could be spelt the same way backwards and forwards. I never did fathom the reasoning behind this, and I might add that 'soapseller' has hardly been a useful addition to my limited vocabulary, except perhaps to provoke more hilarity, and on further consideration, perhaps that was the idea . . .

But Swedish too, is one of the national languages of Finland. This dates from the long period—six hundred years—when Finland was a province of Sweden, and the educated people considered that Finnish was the language of the peasants. The conflict between tongues was another contributive factor to the discords within Finland, making her an even easier prey to the countries on either side, and it is only in very recent times that Finnish has become widely used as a national language. There is still some controversy on this. Swedish speakers claim that the need to learn Finnish for school use holds their children back, while Finnish speakers maintain that the language of Finland should be Finnish and not Swedish. In the south of Finland, where many Swede/Finns live, road and shop signs appear in both languages, but from somewhere about the middle of Hame province the Swedish begins to disappear and people either can't, or won't, speak or understand it. Indeed, it comes sometimes to the point where many Finns prefer to speak English than Swedish, although this is probably also due to the number of English and American programmes on television. I stopped at a garage for petrol about a hundred miles north of Helsinki on one occasion and on seeing my number plates the young lad in charge spoke fluent English. I congratulated him, and asked if he had been in England. 'Oh no,' he replied with a smile. 'It is the television. I have been watching the Forsyte Saga.'

Swedish speakers are inclined to consider the Finnish tongue as *infra dig*, also preferring to use English or German. One morning when I first went to Finland and was having breakfast at my Helsinki hotel, the gentleman at the next table spoke Swedish to the waitress, and then addressed me in very clear English. I do speak some Swedish, but had detected no accent, so asked him from which part of Sweden he came. I was more than a little surprised when he said, 'I am Finnish and very proud to be so. I live near Hanko, but I don't speak the Finnish tongue. I was brought up to speak Swedish and intend to continue to do so.' Nevertheless, when troubles come to Finland, as they have done so often, both factions close ranks and become a nation. We could draw a parallel between this and the way that we in the United Kingdom squabble among ourselves as English, Welsh or Scots, but stand firm when Britain is threatened. It isn't always such a bad thing for a little healthy competition on occasion, provided it isn't allowed to become out of proportion. So, perhaps it can best be summed up by a saying which was popular in Finland at the end of the nineteenth century, just before the emergence of the new nation: 'We are no longer Swedes, we cannot become Russians, let us then be Finns.'

The earliest references to Finland seem to have originated with Tacitus, the Roman historian, in approximately A.D. 100. He referred to a wild primitive people called '*Fenni*' who lived in the Far North without any of the creature comforts that the civilised Romans required as essentials. But that reference could have been to the Lapps. Even now, the Norwegians use the name '*Finner*' when speaking of the inhabitants of Lapland, and one of the Norwegian *fylke* or provinces is called Finnmark. The history of Finland is far older than a mere two thousand years. Along the edges of the Arctic Ocean, where the tundra first appeared after the Ice Age, archaeologists have found relics which prove that a primitive form of human being lived there 8,000 years before the birth of Christ. Only slightly younger are the remains found in southern Finland, for they date from about 7000 B.C. They used stone and bone implements and went in for hunting and fishing, and, because of the very nature of the land and sea at that time, it must have been these people who came from the east. It wasn't quite so difficult in 5000 B.C., because in those days the Finnish climate must have been damp and warm, producing abundant growth, and water chestnuts, now only found in southern climes, grew in the lakes. More humanity migrated northwards . . . the great 'swing to the North' of the day and, because stone weapons have been found from that period made from stones not found in Finland, it is reasoned that there must have been some trading with races from elsewhere. The next arrival was of the pottery people, *circa* 3000 B.C. They are known in the history books as the Comb Ceramic period, because their earthenware vessels have round or tapered bases, decorated with a comblike stamp and again, because they were hunters and fishermen with no domesticated animals except the dog, and even more important, because they had little knowledge of navigation, it is presumed that these Stone Age men had also travelled from the east.

By 1500 B.C. there was another culture. Nowadays known as the Battle-Axe people, because they used boat-shaped battle axes, made from local stone, they were more agriculturally minded, raising cattle and crops, and they were also sailors. It was in this period that the orientation of western Finland turned towards the primitives of Sweden, although in the eastern provinces the links stayed towards the east. Bronze implements are found from that time, but all were imported from east and west and the locals seem to have been quite unaware of their own resources, so widely used today. Then, probably also from the east, came the Finns . . .

It was possibly around the time of the birth of Christ that Rome first found its way to Finland. The Finns had become fur traders by this time, and the Romans needed those skins. Roman swords and wine bowls have been found in Finland, but during the barbarian invasions which followed the fall of Rome, the Finns turned more to the peoples of Scandinavia than to the south and east, for Finnish boat tombs of the period show that they were similar to those used in Scandinavia, the only difference being that they were burned before burial. There is some description of a 'fiery burial in a boat of bronze' in verses from a Finnish folk poem, but there are no written records of this long lost time. Finnish folklore, among the richest in the world, is nowadays called 'Kalevala', after the epic poem written by Elias Lönnrot in the last century, but this poem only contains a fragment of the vast numbers of stories and legends which still exist. Much research is being carried on in this field, in the hope that one day it will throw much needed light into this fascinating and remote period.

Forests and arable land have always been the basis of Finnish economy, even in the distant past, for agriculture required man's attention only in summer, and in spring and autumn he could hunt and fish. Furs provided the main trading currency with foreigners, and it is intriguing to read that the Finnish word for money, *raha*, originally meant 'fur'. When Norwegian and Danish Vikings turned their eyes westwards the Vikings of Sweden travelled to the east, obviously hoping to contact the wealthy Arabian trades, and on their journeyings through Finland furs became an even more important method of barter. Not many Finns bothered to accompany the Vikings eastwards. They preferred to push farther north, to the salmon rivers and game-rich lands of the Lapps, where they proceeded to force the Lapps to pay tribute to them (incidentally, the Swedish Vikings must have met up somewhere with the Arabs because Arabian coins from the sixth century A.D. have been found in the Aland Islands). It is noteworthy too, that the Finnish name for Sweden is 'Ruotsi', presumably from the same root as *Rus*, the name given to Scandinavians travelling the eastern routes in those days, and from which the name Russia is derived. Tradition has it that the Swedish Vikings founded the state of Russia in 862 A.D. It is indeed, an extremely interesting train of thought to pursue . . .

The Finnish instinct for trade is very highly developed, as we see from their startling present-day successes in shipbuilding, textiles, ceramics, and artistic design, as well as in their more traditional fields of woodpulp and timber processing. Oddly enough, the earliest record of the trading activities of the Finns appears in the book produced by our own Alfred the Great. He collected information from all sorts of people in the ninth century, including some from the Norseman Otta. This gentleman had visited the Arctic coasts, and he called the people who lived there 'Kainuans'. They also appear under the name 'Kvenir', in the *Sagas*, so there is double evidence of their existence. In the eleventh century a German chronicler too, Canon Adam of Bremen, tells of an unsuccessful expedition to the 'land of the Kainuu for the purposes of collecting spoils' made by a Prince Anund of Sweden.

By this time the Scandinavian neighbours had formed into three kingdoms, Norway, Sweden and Denmark. But there was no unity between the Finnish tribes. These were, roughly speaking, the Suomalaiset, or proper Finns, in the southeast, whose name gave rise to the nomenclature Suomi, used by Finland today; the Tavastians, or Hamalaiset, lived along the coast and by the western lakes, and their name lives on in the name of the district, Hame; then there were the Karelians, living in the east, along the western side of Lake Ladoga. Each had its own laws, social structures, defence systems, etc. There is evidence of all this in the ancient fortresses which could be manned in time of trouble. But the country was very sparsely populated, with vast stretches of wilderness between the settlements, and while they could all use these hunting grounds, they couldn't defend them. Therein lay the weakness . . . Divide and Rule . . . and so it was to be that, for the next 800 years, Finland was to become an unwilling pawn in the power games practised by the more aggressive neighbours to the east, west and south, and was ruled by Sweden, Germany, Denmark and Russia, before finally declaring herself an independent state on 6 December 1917.

There is complete freedom of worship today in Finland.

Everyone is able to pursue his own beliefs. The Lutheran Church has the largest number of adherents, but there is also an Orthodox Church, a small number of Roman Catholics, and other denominations (as our military services so delightfully put it). Equally, if someone has no beliefs he is welcome to that too. Christianity seems to have arrived in Finland in the eleventh and twelfth centuries, because the names of Findia and Hestia appear in a list of Swedish provinces drawn up for the Pope's benefit in 1120. Quite a lot of legends have sprung up around the man who converted the Finns, and it all points to the fact that he was an Englishman. His name was Henry, and apparently he had been Bishop of Uppsala in Sweden. He went to Finland on a Crusade, organised by King Eric of Sweden, in about 1157. The Bishop was left behind in Finland, presumably to organise his flock, when Eric withdrew his forces, but the unfortunate fellow was killed in the following year by a Finn called Lalli (supposedly a Christian name) on Lake Koylio. He became the patron saint of Turku—this town is also known as Abo—as well as one of the saints of Sweden, and King Eric eventually became the patron saint of Sweden. The cause of Henry's murder isn't clear, but there are certain pointers that the Finns didn't take kindly to the imposition of laws and the cost of building churches, and while happy enough to be Christians when they required help from the Swedes when enemies from Karelia and Russia arrived, they backslid rapidly when the danger was past! So, the Pope advised Sweden to force the Finns into submission by permanently manning the fortresses, but it took them a very long time to do it. Finland became a part of the realm of Sweden, and the union lasted, through many alarums and excursions through the next 600 years, when Sweden, Russia and Germany squabbled over the rich lands of Finland like dogs over a bone. The main effect on the Finnish peoples seems to have been increases in the cost of living. We grumble today, but we haven't yet arrived at the point when, as in the fourteenth century, a loaf of bread cost a cow, and a slice of bread was exchanged for a bull calf. I must say that I hope that this particular piece of history won't repeat itself . . .

The Swedes do, on the whole, seem to have been more popular rulers than the Germans, mainly because the higher noble-
men were by this time, all of Swedish origin. This again explains
the snobbishness inherent in speaking Swedish as a Finn. The
Danes came into the picture when the heir to the Swedish
throne died: Queen Margrethe of Norway and Denmark beat
Albert of Mecklenburg in a battle in the Baltic, so that by 1399
there was a Danish commandant in Turku Castle and the Finns
owed allegiance to the Danish crown. Finnish leaders had been
present at the Kalmar Union ratification in 1397, but as Finland
was not at that time a separate state the constitutional conditions had had little importance for her.

It was while Finland was under Danish rule that the reorganisation of judicial procedures began, which led eventually
to the establishment of a Finnish Supreme Court, so it can be
said that Finland's traditions of autonomy and justice have their
roots in that time. But Finland was still a province of Sweden,
and when the crown went back to Sweden, back went Finland
too. The capital was Turku, and it was here that the first
university of Finland was founded in 1640, just as the first
Finnish language newspapers were printed there by the end of
the eighteenth century. However, as Sweden's power declined,
so Finland became the target for claims from Russia, grown
powerfully in the east, and some of the fiercest fighting was
carried out on her unhappy soil, swaying backwards and forwards across the borders. Russia actually occupied Finland for
eight terrible years, and this period is known in all the history
books as the Great Wrath, synonymous with all that is wretched
and brutal. But again there was a breathing space when the
Russians withdrew in 1721. It was during the Napoleonic Wars
that the final conquest was made. There was a certain amount
of horse-trading between Sweden and Russia . . . 'You leave
Norway to me and I'll give Finland to you' . . . but the Tsar
Alexander I knew that more could be done by giving the Finns
generous conditions rather than weakening his back door, and
so Finland became a Grand Duchy in the Russian Empire in
1809. He moved the capital from Turku to Helsinki in 1812—

it was nearer to Russia and he could keep an eye on things. The constitution was maintained, and a long period of peace followed, and, gradually, there was a change of heart, even among those who had feared Russia most. So much so that when British and French fleets destroyed Russian defences on the Finnish coast during the Crimean War, the Finns were enthusiastically on the Russian side, and, as always, they were doughty fighters.

But the crunch was yet to come. Thanks to the worsening political situation in Europe, Russification of Finland was commenced in 1899, and the peculiarly pleasant position that the Finns had held crumbled from under them. Special petitions went to the Tsar, there were passive resistance campaigns, and refusal to augment new laws, but all to no avail. Then, a young student—Eugene Schauman by name—assassinated the Russian General Bobrikov, who was in effect the Gauleiter of Finland, and a short period of easement ensued, partly due to the Russo/Japanese War. But again the Russian grip tightened and Finland had less and less say in her affairs.

When the First World War broke out, some Finns went to join Germany in the hope that this might be the chance of breaking the Russian stranglehold on their country, but this was by no means considered the best way of attaining the longed for independence. As Finland had had no army of her own since the beginning of the century, Finns were not called upon to shed their blood in the service of Russia, but they did have to provide massive defensive backing, costing millions of marka. However, it wasn't until after the Bolshevik coup in October 1917 that Finland saw her chance. The formal declaration of Independence was made and approved on 6 December 1917, and since then Finland has been a free and independent state in her own right.

Of course that didn't end Finland's troubles. In some ways they were only beginning. Almost immediately there was a civil war, but this time, Finland had leaders of her own who were strong enough to lead. The names of Svinhufvud and Mannerheim will go down into Finnish history. They were vastly different in personality, in looks and in viewpoints, but on one thing they were united. Both were patriots. Both put the welfare of the nation first, believing intensely that their policies were right. And so it was that when Svinhufvud failed when Regent to persuade a German princeling to become the monarchic head of the new Finland and it was obvious that the Germans were going to lose the First World War, Mannerheim took his place as Regent of Finland. Then, after the free election of a new government under a parliamentary system which is in a way similar to Britain's, the United States of America and Britain recognised Finnish independence.

Under a system of free elections which then became part of Finnish life, Finland became a republic, with a president. Retired for a while from public life, but like Churchill in Britain at that time, Mannerheim kept his finger on the pulse of things, for the next decades were to be difficult ones for the new nation. Always looking over her shoulder at the powerful neighbour emerging from the rags and tatters of the Bolshevik Revolution to the east, Finland signed a peace treaty with the Soviets in 1920, whereby the U.S.S.R. also acknowledged her independence and promised to look into the East Karelian position. But this in a way was putting Finland back into the Russian pocket. There was unrest in the west too. The Aland Islands wanted to go back to Sweden, and in 1921 the League of Nations instructed Finland to give the inhabitants local autonomy and keep the area demilitarised. It is ironic in hindsight to see that among the great powers of those days who were the guarantors for the decision the name of U.S.S.R. does not appear. This was to be extremely important, because when in 1938 Sweden agreed to nullify the Aland Pact and strengthen the defences in this area along with Finland, all the signatories, including Germany, agreed, but Russia refused to allow it, and by this time she was a big wheel indeed.

Mannerheim had returned as defence chief when Svinhufvud had been re-elected President, and had stayed in that position even when the ageing president retired, but he had no money to build up the sadly neglected national defences, for Finland was a poor country, needing its finances for so many other things. It wasn't until 1938 that the Finnish Parliament approved the expenditure of money on an arms programme, but by then it was too late to do any good. In 1939, just before the Second World War broke out, thousands of Finns spent their summer vacations working like beavers to strengthen the fortifications along the Karelian Isthmus, for, as can well be appreciated, the Finns had long learned to expect attack from the east. But still they hoped against hope to stay neutral in the face of the inevitable storms ahead; hoping too that the u.s.s.r. would not become involved, but looking askance at the Non-Aggression pact with Nazi Germany . . .

These hopes were of course completely dashed when Soviet troops crossed in overwhelming numbers on 30 November 1939. It looked as though Finland was doomed, and indeed resistance might not have been so fierce if Stalin had not tried to set up a puppet Finnish government in readiness to take over. Everything that the Finns had fought for so long and so bitterly was now endangered. In a famous order, Mannerheim referred to it as 'Everything the Finnish people held dear and sacred', and so they fought again, a lion cub against a full-grown bear. They appealed to the League of Nations, but this now sterile organisation could do nothing except expel Russia from its dwindling numbers. World sympathy wasn't much help against bullets. And still the resistance of the young lion was fanatical, and at one time it even looked as though it might win . . . only that the sheer weight of the bear must make the outcome inevitable if help from outside was not forthcoming.

Even now, when one meets men who took part in that bitter, tragic, glorious war, one feels the surging pride. The survivors are of course, an ageing generation. I remember sitting one summer evening in a hotel in Hanko, in southern Finland, talking to a mountain of a man who had had his face half shot away at Lake Ladoga. He talked with difficulty, but with passion, and as he talked, it was very easy to understand why, such a short time later, when the Finns saw that Germany was declaring war on the u.s.s.r., they joined battle again, hoping against hope that they might regain their territories. 'We are always on the losing side'—I have heard this time and time again, often said with a wry smile. They had indeed backed the wrong horse, and perhaps the greatest irony of all the Finns' tragic struggles for self-determination as a nation was the moment when, at the behest of the victorious Soviet Union, allied with the Western Powers, they had to turn round and drive their erstwhile comrades of Nazi Germany from Finnish soil. Still more tragedy was to come, for, as they retreated, the Germans set fire to all Lapland. Not one village, one town, was left standing one stone upon the other. Senseless, vengeful destruction, but that is the true face of war, as it has been known throughout the centuries to all mankind.

The enormous reparations that the u.s.s.r. demanded from Finland meant that she had to find some way of making money quickly, for the monies were set at prewar prices. Sweden helped as generously as possible. Factories were set up, metal industries and shipbuilding yards developed, because much of the reparation had to be in kind, but the people themselves accepted a much lower standard of living to do it. It was, after all, a point of honour. At the same time, they had to cope with a huge influx of refugees from Karelia, who had refused to stay within the new u.s.s.r. borders, which incidentally included the nickel mines at Petsamo. Mannerheim, now an old man, resigned and Passikivi took his place.

The new industries which had been built at such cost were to prove the salvation of the nation, for, after completely fulfilling the u.s.s.r.'s demands, Finland was able to turn her thoughts towards exporting in trade, not only to Iron Curtain countries, but to the western world. But they tread warily: they walk a tightrope between east and west. Their neutrality has, by dint of long and patient negotiations, been accepted in good faith by the majority of the rest of the world. There are considerable restrictions on certain things they would like to try, but they cannot afford to argue too strongly with, nor completely offend the u.s.s.r. But, at the same time, they have said a firm 'no' on more than one occasion. Their press, television and radio are 'free', but they do exercise a measure of self-censorship. I think that if there came to be matters on which the Finns felt very strongly indeed they would state their views courageously. After all, that is a virtue which this nation has been proved to possess in abundance. I have talked to many Finns in many political parties on how they feel. Apart from the dyed-in-the-wool Communist, and there are of course, some of these, many are sure that their position will be respected because, as one woman put it, 'we are a convenient bridge between East and West'. Others say that they are always prepared that one day they may wake up in the morning to find that they are 'being hugged by a bear'. But all, without exception, Communist or not, have been proud to be Finns. As I said at the beginning of this potted history lesson, they cannot choose their neighbours. But they prefer to live in amity with them. After the superhuman struggles they have made for generations, no man could doubt their right so to do.

In the postwar struggle for self determination, albeit that the self determination is of a slightly restricted kind, tourism has undoubtedly helped considerably, for it is attempting to show that the Finnish people want the world to visit them in friendship, from wheresoever the visitors might come. And too, it is worth mentioning here that the fact that one can get a visa-free trip into the u.s.s.r. from Finland has helped many people from the west to get a closer look at the enigma of Russia, always a step towards understanding one hopes, so that Finland has become in a way, a 'Gateway through the Curtain'. Within Finland, tourist publicity has been good, brochures and books thoughtfully and artistically produced, souvenirs are seldom trash, and tourist boards, transport systems, travel agencies, hoteliers and the like have put a great deal of combined effort into supplying the tourist's needs, albeit it not exactly at the cheap end of the tourist market. In any large hotel in Helsinki, and increasingly across Finland too, one finds guests from Peking and Philadelphia, Calcutta and Cologne, Japan or Jordan, Israel or Italy, all eating within close proximity and in apparent amity. This can't be bad. It has all been done with the Finns' natural flair for understatement and with no banging of big drums, for the eternally practical Finns are realists, knowing that they cannot be all things to all men when it comes to the requirements of the world's holidaymakers, but they have a tremendous amount to give to people interested enough to make the long journey to see for themselves.

Welcome to Finland—*Tervetuala Suomeen*—the first words I heard on Finnish soil. If this book helps to bring just a little of the warmth of that welcome, together with a modicum of knowledge of this fascinating country to its readers, it will have served its purpose.

2. Getting To, and Around, Finland

One can arrive in Finland from Europe in five ways. By air, by sea, by road, in trains, or on one's two feet. I have travelled to Finland by each method. But I would hasten to add that I only walked across the bridge linking Tornio in Finland and Haparanda in Sweden, for the sake of being able to claim that I had actually arrived on foot! I then went back and drove across in style, and as there are no customs formalities at borders within Scandinavia, it raised not even an eyebrow. Whichever way one chooses to go, it is quite a long journey, even from within Scandinavia, for distances are considerable and deceptive. But all the ways are interesting and sometimes very beautiful.

The very first time I went to Helsinki I travelled by ship from Copenhagen in midsummer, when the Baltic was bluer than the Mediterranean, and many passengers slept on the decks for the few hours of darkness instead of in their air-conditioned cabins. The northern seas are surprising in this respect. I've had more rough weather in southern waters than in the oft-maligned northern ones, but when it does blow, there are no half measures. On that occasion when nearing Finland, we threaded our way through the rocky islands of the Archipelago, some of them deserted, but many with small cottages, a flagpole and a sauna by the edge of the water, and many happy mortals were playing with boats, fishing or swimming; then, as we passed the Suomenlinna fortress fortifications, Helsinki was in front of us, a grey and white façade, with the dome of the Cathedral standing greenly behind it, and the 'onions' of the Greek Orthodox Uspenki Cathedral to the right. There were a few people about, but not many, for it was a sweltering Saturday afternoon, and unless there is vital business afoot, Helsinki folk, like the rest of Scandinavia, go to ground in their summer houses on Friday evening and don't reappear until Monday morning. There was something exotic about the city on that day, and I remember thinking that it was entirely different from any other Scandinavian town or city that I had ever seen.

Another time I came from Stockholm in winter, and we had little sleep on the ship because of the thunderous noise made by the ice, breaking before the thrust of our specially strengthened bow. This time, the islands were lonely in their winter cocoon of ice. But in the early light, Helsinki waterfront was still grey and white and slightly exotic-looking, even with the lights of the car headlamps illuminating the slush. Pedestrians, formless in their heavy winter clothes, waited on the quay as we docked, stamping their feet or seeking the warmth of the terminal buildings while their friends disembarked. Between these extremes of climate, the sailors on these ships have a year of sea travel and weather wisdom. Regular ferry services connect Finland with Sweden, Denmark, Germany and England, as well as with the U.S.S.R. and Estonia. All of them are clean, good and comfortable, and all the fleets are constantly under review to keep their standards of safety and seamanship at the highest level. Nowadays the ships are highly modern and offer in my view some of the best value for money among ferry services anywhere. They have spotlessly clean accommodation, excellent food and lively bars, entertainment, swimming pools, and of course sauna. The self-service shops on some of them are very well stocked. These always provide a great attraction, for the cost of alcohol is extremely high in all the Scandinavian countries. I always wait to board the ferries before buying my much prized bottles of Finnish liqueurs and Finnish chocolates on the way home, joining the queues of 'locals' who seem to be buying the whole ship. Stockholmers in particular use the ferries to Finland a lot for their shopping expeditions into Finland. The cost of many commodities (meat in particular) is less in Finland than in Sweden and I have derived a good deal of

1, 2 Two aspects of the Sibelius Monument, Helsinki, designed by Eila Hiltunen

3   *The Cathedral, Senate Square, Helsinki, designed by Gustav Engel*

amusement by sitting quietly at dinner on a journey westwards and listening to the housewives discussing their 'good buys' and even producing the meat for inspection! They do the same thing on the ferries from south Sweden into Denmark, and I must admit that I have joined the expeditions on occasion. Swedish people maintain that they can even save enough to pay for their trip and enjoy the weekend away into the bargain, much as so many continentals make sorties into England to visit 'Marks and Sparks' and Sainsbury's . . . Isn't it an odd quirk of human nature? But it all makes profits for the ferry operators, wherever they may ply.

Suomen Hoyrylaiva Osakeyhtio/Finska Angfartygs/Aktiebolaget/Finland Steamship Company Limited—to give it its name in Finnish, Swedish and English, was started in 1883 while Finland was still an autonomous state under Russia. One of the main reasons for its establishment was the need to find a method of transport for the export of butter from Finland to Hull, but naturally other routes were added as well as charter tours in winter, going out to Las Palmas, the West Indies and u.s.a. Immigrants too formed a large part of the trade. But it wasn't all one way: I was fascinated to see a travel brochure from 1904 published by the company, which advertised 'package tours' in Finland. It quoted from an article in *The Traveller* of 8 September 1900: 'You are tired of Switzerland, overrun by tourists of every nationality in the world; you are weary of Norway for the same reason; you have had enough of the "cure" with its eternal waters and baccarat and you want to get away from the bustle and the gaiety of the continental seaside resort. Where shall you go? Why not try Finland?' and went on to extol the forests, the hunting and the fishing, the good food on the ships, the trains and the fresh air. Have you ever had the feeling that your job is somewhat superfluous? I did!

In 1904 a twelve-day package tour, first class, including voyage, hotel and meals in Helsinki, cost £11 10s. Second class was £7 5s od and in 1912 you could, according to another brochure, travel from Hull to Helsinki, Hanko or Turku for £6 return. When one takes into account the difference in the value of money between those days and the present, it would seem that the shipping lines have kept the prices to a reasonable level, and in some ways improved upon them, for certainly conditions and comfort are at a higher standard now, along with the costs.

There was a *Titania* once, in the fleet. Built by Gourley Brothers of Dundee, and delivered in 1908, she was the pride of the line for eight years, but then, alas, she was requisitioned by the British Admiralty in the First World War, on 14 March 1916, and almost exactly two years later, on 28 March 1918, hit a mine and sank off the Scottish east coast. She was registered as 3,490 tons and had 739 berths. The present flagship, *Finlandia*, one of the prettiest car ferry ships one can find, has a tonnage of 8,200 and 647 berths, but can take 900 passengers. She travels between Travemunde in Germany via Copenhagen to Helsinki, and therefore one has to get either to Germany or to Denmark to board her, but when I made a voyage on her I reckoned it was worth the effort, for as I was the only English passenger aboard on that trip I was looked after as if I was the Queen, and not just her humble subject.

Nowadays, the direct holiday links between Finland and Britain are maintained by Finnlines from Felixstowe and London, with drive-on ships. These are part of the fleet of an extremely prosperous shipping line which was established as recently as 1947. Like much else in Finland, it was founded in determination. The Second World War had decimated Finnish commercial shipping and without ships the export programme on which it was obvious that Finland would depend for survival could not be carried through. So, some of the largest industrial and wholesale concerns invested money together and established Merivienti Oy (*oy* means 'company') and Oy Finnlines Limited. Merivienti Oy started with six very elderly ships. *Willie*, their first, started life in 1923 as *Helmwood* and was built in Barrow by Vickers and had had a spell, like all good sailors, sailing out of Shanghai under the name of *Hai Pung*, before joining the Finns. Her life wasn't finished after her usefulness to them ceased either, for she wandered the world for a lot longer before being scrapped at Hamburg. On such ships are

the histories and reputations of the great shipping lines of the
the world founded . . . Nowadays, Finnlines are among the
most forward-looking of companies, and indeed by 1977 they
hope to have a gas turbine passenger liner in service between
Travemunde in West Germany, and Helsinki. *Finnjet*, as the
ship will be called, will be built in Wartsila's yard at Helsinki,
where an increasing number of the world's most modern ships
are finding their birthplace. All of this is a very long way from
the Hull butter run . . .

You can also travel across the breast of Sweden and join Silja
Line, which plies between Stockholm and Norrtalje, to Helsinki
and Turku. Silja is a consortium comprising three companies:
Bore of Turku, Svea Line of Stockholm and (of course!)
Finland Steamship Co. of Helsinki. The name Silja was chosen
because it has connotations both in Sweden and in Finland.
There is a beautiful area in Sweden called Siljan, and Silja is
the name of a girl in a famous Finnish novel by the Nobel
prizewinner Sillanpaa. Viking Line sails between Kapellskar/-
Mariehamn and Naantali, stopping in the Aland Islands,
which have such a special place in Swedish and Finnish history,
and which are well worth a stopover. Other methods of transport across the Gulf of Bothnia are the pleasant Wasa Line,
operating from Umea and Sundsvall to Vaasa and Pori, or
Jacob Lines, from Umea and Skelleftea to Pietasaari (Jacob-
stad) and these connections can be very useful when one is
making an extended tour in Scandinavia. For instance, by
going north in Norway as far as Mo-i-Rana, one can take the
'yellow road' to Umea across Sweden, and proceed to Finland
from there, coming back by one of the other routes already
mentioned. It is always noticeable that in the Mo-i-Rana area
of Norway one sees many more Finnish numberplates on the
cars, and it follows that this is a very popular route among the
Finns themselves. All these ferries take cars, caravans etc., so
traffic is well catered for, but in high season it might be advisable to book ahead.

Road and train links from the west must, of geographical
necessity, use the shipping links from Hamburg, Copenhagen

or Stockholm, but one can also come into Finland via northern Sweden and northern Norway, and I will deal with these later.

We rather take air travel for granted in this day and age, but I never fail to derive a great deal of pleasure from travelling long distances over Scandinavia by air because, so often, even in winter, the skies are clear enough to see every detail of the lands below. Arrival over Finland in winter often means that the long low horizon looks like an iced Christmas cake from which some of the icing has fallen away, while the islands off the coastline form dark crumbs on the grey-white porcelain that is the frozen Baltic. In summer, one has the feeling of descending to a long-haired richly patterned, dark green and blue carpet, where some child has spilled handfuls of brown and white Minibricks before being carried off for tea, while the Baltic looks like speckled blue and white linoleum. Fanciful? Perhaps, for inside almost every air traveller there is a poet struggling to express his opinion of the vistas spreading below him, but most of us are afraid to comment aloud.

Air travel has certainly cut down the time needed to get to and from Finland in drastic fashion. One can catch the 13.40 Finnair flight from London Airport and be in the pleasant, modern, unpretentious Helsinki air terminal in two hours fifty minutes, although thanks to the eastern time operating in Finland, the clocks will register 17.30. On the return journey, a departure of 09.10 from Helsinki arrives in London at 11.10, which does help a business man to snatch a clear business afternoon, but perhaps that isn't always an unmitigated advantage! Many international airlines operate directly into Helsinki, including British Airways, who have a pool service with Finnair.

Birthdays are something rather special in Finland, as elsewhere in Scandinavia, and notices of congratulation appear in daily papers. I've always felt that this was a little ungallant to the fair sex to say the least, but I have been assured on very good authority that it is not unknown for a lady to have several 35th birthdays—suitably spread, naturally. But when Finnair celebrated its 50th birthday in 1973, there was no need for

reticence. Indeed it was something to be proud of. It was on
1 November 1923 that the Aero Oy was founded, thanks mainly
to the foresight and energies of Bruno Lucander and the fact
that he had a long and personal friendship with Professor
Junker, the designer of the great German aircraft of the same
name. The Aero Oy of Finland, or Finnair, as it later became,
made its first commercial passenger flight on 20 March 1924,
between Helsinki and Tallin, with a Junkers F13. There were
four passengers, for that was all that the plane could hold.

For the first years of Finnair's existence, the flying was
seasonal, because their planes were equipped with skis in
winter and floats in summer, but of course, they couldn't take
off when the ice was forming or breaking up; by 1936 the
Junkers fleet were fitted with wheels, and they flew from
Malmi. Now, fifty years later, Finnair is the sixth oldest in the
hundred-odd members of IATA and flies worldwide.

But worldwide travel is a bit commonplace now and is just
another facet of the modern scene. For me there is much more
interest in the seventeen or so small airports scattered across
the length and breadth of Finland, for travelling by aircraft
has given a new dimension to the country Finn, previously
often isolated by weather conditions for weeks. This is of course
a dimension which has become general throughout Norway,
Sweden and Finland and the number of small light planes to
be found throughout these countries is very high and still
growing fast, so that it is not so unusual for Scandinavian
families living in isolated areas to have a plane instead of, and
often in addition to, a car and a boat. Some of my own happiest
hours have been spent in the cockpit of a friend's private plane
and certainly I've learned a great deal more about the terrain
of the north that way. One is inclined to take much more of a
personal interest in landmarks when the weather is bad, even
though the radio is in constant communication with beacons
and airfields. In Finland detailed information can be had from
the Finnish Aviation Association, who have published an
excellent little book in English about radio, beacons, airfields,
etc., for private flying is used extensively both for business and

pleasure and there are a number of good charter and air taxi firms available. This, not unnaturally, costs money. But like everything else, it depends on one's requirements, priorities and pocket.

For the tourist within Finland, Finnair's domestic air routes are a good way of seeing more of the country, for one does get quite an insight into national characteristics by just travelling beside ordinary folk on regular air, bus and train services. I still get quite a kick from finding a Lapp in full national dress waiting beside me on an airport far beyond the Arctic Circle, even though there is always a faint disappointment when he climbs into a DC9 instead of a pulkka! Air fares are quite reasonable for the distances covered, and in addition there are many concessions for visitors, including unlimited holiday tickets and family discounts etc., and one must hope that these will continue in spite of the worldwide fuel problems. At the time of writing, in line with the national policies of trying to promote tourism within Finland there are also some rather special excursions run by Finnair which have become firm favourites with foreign visitors. Of these I'd single out particularly the Midnight Sun flights. These run for the two months of midsummer when the sun never sets in Lapland. The trip goes from Helsinki to Rovaniemi by air, and from there passengers are taken to the hotel on Ounasvaara fell, fed on Lapland delicacies like Arctic salmon, reindeer stew and cloudberries, suitably entertained (which of course in Finland inevitably includes a sauna, taken in the wee sma' hours) and brought back to Helsinki. If you are lucky the sun will have shone all the time and on Midsummer night itself, thousands of bonfires glow along the lakeshores far below you as you wing your way northwards between Helsinki and Rovaniemi.

This excursion is particularly popular with visitors from the United States, who always make up a considerable proportion of the tourist figures in Finland. Many Finns emigrated to the States in the last half of the nineteenth century and their descendants frequently come back to see where their roots lie. Indeed, within the Finnish element of the United States population, traditions and customs of the old country are still firmly upheld, and they continue to speak an Americanised brand of Finnish. When touring in Finland, one often meets quite elderly people who remember being taken as children to the New World, and, after having spent a lifetime there, come back during their retirement years, just to see for themselves. It is about two years since I travelled from Turku to Norrtalje with four delightful Canadians, all in their sixties. The two men were brothers whose Finnish parents had taken them to live in the United States when they were little. From there the family had moved north to Canada and, when the boys grew up, they went to work in separate places. But they both married girls with Scandinavian backgrounds, one a second generation Canadian with Swedish parentage, and the other a Finnish girl, almost straight off the emigrant boat. And there they all were, making the grand tour of places they had longed to see, finding relations who had only been names on a Christmas letter, visiting farms and villages where their families had lived for generations, and using the half familiar tongue of their parents, with which they had been brought up. They all told me they had loved every moment and only wished they had come years before.

'Could you live in Finland now?' I asked one of the brothers. He hesitated a while before replying. 'I'm not sure,' he said slowly. 'I've been brought up to think as a Canadian, but our home life has always been in the Finnish pattern, celebrating the traditional things, like Pikkujoulu for instance.' I nodded, knowing that he referred to Little Christmas, and he went on, 'I went on vacation to quite a lot of places when my kids were growing up, but here, in Finland, this is where I have felt I was a part of the land and of the people. It's all a question of background perhaps, and I guess I'd find it kind of hard to settle in Finland now, but there must be something in blood being thicker than water. I liked it, and I think it liked me. The pace isn't so hard,' and with a laugh 'all our relations seem to be living quite old! But I guess it's too late now. I'd find it hard to change back in some ways . . .' He fell silent and his wife joined in, 'I liked it too and I loved every one of my relations, and I'm coming back, just as often as I can until I'm too old to travel any more, but our kids are in Canada—so that's where we'll stay . . .'

Apart from Finnair there is the diminutive Sir-Air Oy, which operates both commercial and scheduled flights. Most of its aircraft are Pipers, and apart from its wide use by business executives, the company arranges mercy flights and is used quite extensively by tourists wanting their own pet plane transport. It's certainly not a cheap way of getting around Finland, but when one compares it with rates elsewhere in the world for flights of this kind, it can look positively bargain basement, but how long this can continue under present world fuel pressures is anyone's guess.

Whenever I go to the huge railway station in the centre of Helsinki and make my way on to the platforms to catch a train, I am much more conscious of the 'Eastern European' flavour of Finland. Particularly is this so in winter. It is almost impossible to explain the sensation. It may be derived from the fact that one has to clamber up the high steps into the train— it may be purely due to the fact that here one has more time to see the individual faces of the dark-coated, fur-capped men, or the tall-booted, leather- or fur-clad women, or even perhaps the little everyday lady in the respectable black coat, whose face bears the unmistakable Slavonic ancestry is the reason, rather than the inevitable crop of dungareed youngsters with long hair and haunted eyes that one finds everywhere, and not only in Finland. But the feeling of being on the 'edge' of Scandinavia stays with me, whether the train is going to Turku or Tampere, Porvoo or Pieksämäki. Perhaps it is due instead to the trolley of drinks and sweets which are pushed through the day train by a stout body in a white coat! It's all rather far removed from British Rail and its perky stewards.

Some trains are still without restaurant cars or buffets so this often results in being surrounded by an assortment of picnic baskets. Why is it that immediately the train moves from its starting place the whistle is also the signal for everyone to be

seized with a desire to eat? And what's more, to continue to
do so right to their destination? It seems to be a universal
human trait; I don't mind it when I've come armed with my
own picnic, so it is rather a case of green cheese, but I mention
the fact in this connection only because one should find out,
before going on a Finnish train, whether there is a restaurant
car or not, and go prepared accordingly! A day's travel can
be very tiring if there isn't even the little stout body in the white
coat to relieve the ennui!

The same rule applies to overnight trains. Find out if there
is going to be a dining car on your sleeper north (or south). The
journey can be a long slow business with stops at every station
en route, or so it seems. Last spring I caught a night train to
Rovaniemi on my way to ski in Lapland. The train was spotlessly clean, the corridors carpeted, the loos impeccable and
the bunks exceedingly roomy in my sleeper, but try as I might,
I could find no coach where one could go and sit for a while
before retiring. Instead, there were little jump seats placed
outside the sleeping accommodation, of the type one used to
find in the London Underground. So, after perching there for
a bit and swaying like a budgie on a swing, I tried peering out
of the window beside my sleeping berth, with my head wedged
under the base of the upper bunk. I gave up the unequal
struggle and went to bed early. A hostess came along and took
orders for beer, sandwiches and coffee, with a repeat order for
the following morning, and I must admit that I longed for
British Rail's morning tea! My consolation was that I'd had
an early night, but next time I'll take extra reading material
and perhaps one of the despised picnics. There will eventually
be more restaurant cars but these things take time in Finland.

One consolation is that the fares on Finnish trains are very
reasonable, particularly for foreigners, who can get a Finnrail
pass with unlimited rail travel, and too there are combined
train/air/bus/inland boat tickets. I've never tried to use one of
these, but according to my more hardy friends they work very
well. You can also put your car and/or caravan on the train to

Kemi, Oulu and Rovaniemi at very reasonable cost. Again, a great help if there is only a limited amount of time to spare.

You'll need slightly more than a 'limited' amount of time if you intend to take a long-distance post bus in Finland, but to be absolutely fair this comment only applies to the non-express ones. There is a fine system of express buses, and they really cover the mileage in grand style. They link with train and air services, and are included in the ubiquitous Finnrail tickets I've just referred to. But it is my firm and unshakeable opinion that everyone who visits Finland must travel at least once on the non-express bus to complete his education. Once might be enough for you. I've done it several times now, but then, I'm a glutton for punishment . . .

All the country buses, whether express or non, work on the excellent premise that they are there for the service of the public and not the other way around. They await the arrival of trains, or aircraft, or boats, and in outlying districts there is a delightful system whereby people ring the bus office the night before to make sure that the driver on the early run knows that he has to wait for passengers at some certain point. I've known him to sound the horn at some distance off, to announce his arrival, just to make sure that they don't need to wait outside on some bitter morning. This is rather refreshing to someone used to the 'ring the bell and go regardless' attitude of many a London Transport conductor. But of course, it is understandable when perhaps there may not be another bus for hours, or even a day.

The drill for catching a bus is similar all over the world, but at the back of all the long-distance buses in Finland there is a large area reserved for such things as bicycles, prams, garden implements, skis, packages of all shapes and sizes and your luggage, so you go there first and deposit your cases, then round to the front and get in. As in the train, a hook for coats is placed above the seat, as well as a rack. This can be a bit of a hazard for the curious who want to see out and have to peer round the macintoshes or furs—most passengers know the route only too well I suppose. The interior of the bus is warm, because the engines are perpetually running, but the door stays open, which can be quite a hardship while waiting on a cold winter's morning. Most people start to hang up their top coats immediately on arrival on board. It would be rather difficult to keep them all on for the seats are distinctly on the small side. (I'm always strongly reminded of the little sign we used to see in London buses: 'we are trying to get you wider seats on your bus', and wish it had occurred to the bus-owners in Finland too.)

After about a quarter of an hour, or maybe longer, most people seem to have arrived, but the bus still waits, its engine purring patiently. Then comes the *pièce de résistance*. There is a small seat beside the driver, plus a large space which is obviously for luggage, or so I thought. I was soon disabused of this idea and was banished, quite politely but firmly to the rear space already mentioned—that is why I say there is a drill for Finnish buses. The front area is for the newspapers and for the mail, and the small seat is for the postman-cum-newspaperman-cum-conductor. When he arrives on this particular morning he looks just like the rest of us in his heavy civilian coat, but hey presto, he removes it and his suit jacket, dons his uniform and picks up his heavy conductor's pouch and ticket gadget, and is transformed into all his roles like the prince in the pantomime. He makes a cursory inspection of his assorted clutch of expressionless passengers, his post and his newspapers, which by now, are overflowing on to the limited floor space by the door, nods to his driver, and the bus doors hiccup to a close as we start off across the crunching snow and slush of the station yard towards the outskirts of Rovaniemi.

Act One begins. He becomes the bus conductor, and brings his impedimenta on a lurching journey around the bus. By the time he's finished with all of us, we've picked up more passengers at odd stops, the houses are thinning out, and there are signs of open country ahead, where the grey of the morning is giving way to lighter skies and a magpie or two on a bare tree. Ah, one thinks, now the bus will get moving. It bumbles along steadily enough, but would hardly win prizes for speed.

Act Two. The conductor transforms himself into the newsboy

and postman simultaneously, a remarkable feat, and has dumped his conductor's props on the bench beside him. He's untying bundles of newspapers and letters and placing the letters inside the individual copies of newspapers, stopping, like postmen the world over, to read the postcards. All these are in some order known only to him, and the reason for this soon becomes obvious. The bus crawls now, the door hiccups open and Mercury, as I have dubbed him, stands on the low step above the snow, leans far out and throws the newspaper and its contents into the waiting mouth of a small box on the roadside. Who for? There's not a house in sight. Oh yes, there it is, away across two snowy fields. I reflect that if he is going to do this all the way to Enontekio I'm in for a long sit, and wish I hadn't chosen the seat by the door after all. The boxes on the road come thick and fast, which is more than the bus is, and the performance is repeated again and again. We stop too, for passengers. A middle aged lady, shapeless in her thick coat and woolly hat. A young girl, surprisingly lightly clad for she looks like any other teenager with her long hair, jeans and thin sweater topped by a fur-trimmed leather coat, but she has wellingtons in place of fashion boots and heavy tights in place of the thin nylon ones, for they are useless in this Finnish winter of the north. There's a farmhand in blue lumber jacket and cap, whose high-cheeked, pale skinned face contrasts strangely with his heavy work-grained hands. There's an old man, who reeks of spirits even at this early hour; children of all ages, making their way to school, noisy, chattering, fighting as kids will all over the world; the kaleidoscope changes, yet the pattern remains. Post, newspapers, people, stop, start; then the bus jerks on to a side road, leaving the comparatively clear main roads for a bumpy farm track. When it stops it is within sight of a large house on a small incline, and our Mercury steps out in his light trousers and shoes, plunging off into the rotten snow with his bundles of good and bad news and disappears into a doorway, returning, some little while on, with something which looks suspiciously like a cakebox. On the bus, and off again with a nod and a brief comment to his driver. I notice that as he

continues to sort the mail he always looks closely at the stamps
—perhaps he collects them and asks his customers for them.
Back to the main road, and on . . .

In another two hours, when the novelty of the journey has
completely worn off and I'm beginning to envy the inner warmth
of the old chap who had had the foresight to fortify himself with
aquavit, the bus rumbles into a little hamlet and comes to a
standstill outside a small *kahvlia*. The conductor announces
something which I don't understand and everybody struggles
into coats and proceeds to shamble off the bus. I ask in Swedish
(I'd tried English earlier) and he shrugs his shoulders and looks
hopefully at his mate, who nods briefly and replies in Swedish
that we get a quarter of an hour here for coffee. The café is
crowded and very reminiscent of a Wild West saloon, brought
up to date. No bartender, no alcohol, but the faces are somehow
very much the same. But the coffee is good, and so are the open
sandwiches. I see the aquavit man is drinking beer. Perhaps I
ought to follow suit? Out of the corner of my eye I see Mercury
and his coachman picking up the money pouch. Must be time
to go. A quick visit to the loo and out to join the other passengers, shuffling to board the bus, which now seems redolent of
diesel oil and cigarette smoke; didn't notice it so much before.

The countryside slips past in endless vistas of black and white,
the far-off hills sometimes tinted with violet and blue and tipped
in the pale sun with gold. Villages where the small houses fade
into the landscape except for the brilliance of the flowers tucked
snugly inside their double glazing, or a snowcat discarded like
a child's toy, near a gate. Often there are ridges of snow built
across the cleared surfaces of the road, and one wonders idly
what they are for. Then one catches a sight of someone using
one. They are to take these very snowcats or sledges across the
roads, because they won't run on the bared surfaces—ingenious.
Snowcats have revolutionised the existence of the people living
in the north, particularly the Lapps, but in spite of their un-
doubted benefits, one can't help being thankful that tourists
are not allowed to use them—yet.

Still we stop at every farm gate, at every sub post office, but,

by the time I get to my stop, where I must take a taxi to my
final destination (I still marvel that hired car services can make
enough money to live on in these more desolate spots, when one
compares the life of the taximan in the metropolises of the world)
the newspaper pile is down to a handful, and the letters, merely
a dozen or so, lying forlornly on the erstwhile busy sorting
place. The cakebox has been joined by other mysterious things,
the conductor has eaten a sandwich from yet another package,
chatted to the driver, who has hitherto silently manipulated
his bus across the Arctic, passengers have struggled into their
coats, collected their belongings from the back of the bus, and
descended into the clean thin air of the country, and all with
very few words passing between any of them. But for part of
the way I have been talking to a charming elderly lady from
Helsinki, who tells me that she spends part of every winter up
here in the north, and that she always travels on the postal bus.
'I see the people,' she says, 'and they, at least, don't change in
this changing world.'

I've been on several of these buses now, and she was quite
right. The people don't change. Only the seasons do that. For
a new dimension in thought, to see the people and the places
as my Helsinki lady does, the journey is marvellous, and fun.
But I can better understand the early morning fortification
with aquavit. I might be tempted to join that league too if I
had to do that journey by compulsion instead of choice. As it
is, I'll go again as soon as I can, if only to find out where the
conductor finally delivers his cakeboxes!

One of the easiest and pleasantest ways of travelling to and
within Finland is by car, for obviously it is very satisfactory to
have one's own car at one's disposal. I've always found it well
worth while to take my car with me, travelling across Denmark
or Sweden and then all over Finland, but it does take extra
time to do this, and for the holidaymaker who has only a limited
time and wants to spend every moment in Finland itself and
not necessarily to enjoy the other Scandinavians too, delectable
as they may be, it is not the best solution. But for someone who
has to travel in Finland for some weeks, and who is prepared to

put a spurt on through Denmark or Sweden or Germany, or go by sea direct from Britain, then one's own car is helpful.

There are in any case plenty of reputable local car-hire firms, as well as agencies for the big European ones, and prices are comparable with elsewhere. In many ways this is the better, though costlier, system for it does mean that the wear and tear is not on one's own precious vehicle, and as Finland, in common with the rest of Europe and Scandinavia, drives on the right, it is less limiting in vision to have a car with lefthand drive. Within the towns and cities, there is quite a lot of traffic, particularly at rush hours, and one has to watch for tram tracks too, which get a bit slippery in wet weather. Some of the busiest out-of-town roads are around Helsinki, and in summer particularly, the road to Porvoo can take quite a long time to negotiate. But once through these areas, roads have little traffic and one travels for miles without meeting another vehicle apart from the occasional farm tractor or a mother pushing a pram.

Main roads are on the whole slightly wider than ours, and surfaces are mostly asphalt or oil and sand. Country roads often leave a lot to be desired. In the south roads follow the contours of the lakes, so that there are endless vistas of water, trees and farms to please the eye. Many roads run quite straight for miles, so that one can see the landscape as well as driving; there isn't therefore the same strain on the driver as on more tortuous routes. But road repairs have to be accomplished in the very short summer months, and one is likely to suddenly 'run out of road' and bump unhappily over a series of potholes, ruts and gravel to an accompaniment of encouraging comments from the roadmenders—they are a universal breed in all countries, I find—for a mile or two before rejoining a surfaced section. To be fair, there are always signs which indicate the possibility of this state of affairs, and in the southern half of Finland they appear in Swedish and in Finnish. But, as one penetrates further north, Finnish often appears alone, without international signals, and it isn't always possible to have found out what '*Ajo Sallittu Omalla Vastuulla*' means in the phrasebook before you are locked in combat with it, and discover that it says, and *means*, 'Driving permitted at own risk'! Every driver must have ' *Tietyo*' engraved on his heart as translating 'roadworks'!

Main roads are also kept open and cleared all year in the face of very fierce weather. It is a pretty impressive achievement for a small country, particularly when one's mind's eye remembers what one inch of snow does to the mentality of British drivers. Naturally, it costs a lot of money. Nearly £3,000,000 was spent on general maintenance alone in 1971, the latest year on which I was able to get figures, but it also provides a lot of casual work when unemployment is still a big problem in Finland. Some money is expended annually on the building of motorways too, but at the moment there is only one of these, stretching for about thirty kilometres from Helsinki to Espoo, deluding the newcomer into thinking that there must be much more, and the exits to some of the main towns have often got a few hundred yards of wide road which show where the motorways will eventually run. It is a beginning after all, and with such a small, scattered population, more seems hardly necessary at the present time. It is really very pleasant the way it is, apart from the rather steep camber in the centre of the roads; but then, I have never been a creature of change.

Driving in towns presents little difficulty, provided you keep to the rules and make it clear where you want to go, for on the whole local drivers are tolerant, and even considerate, of a foreigner's antics. There is a dearth of traffic lights, but a wealth of directional road signs, so providing all occupants of the car keep eyes peeled and you position accordingly, all should be well. You'll soon get used to the fact that most Finns drive with their lights on, particularly in bad weather. There are plenty of service stations and garages, but in the country districts there may be long distances between them, and then it is advisable to carry a spare can of petrol with you. Perhaps I should mention too, that one comes unsuspectingly to ferry crossings. On the lakeside and island roads, it can be quite disconcerting to suddenly arrive at a stretch of water, when the gap is widening between you and the boat! There are always warnings, but again, when one is wrapped in the scenery, struggling to read

4   'Sauna . . . It is almost another religion.'

5   *The Civic Theatre, Helsinki*

6   *The entrance to the Congress Halls, Dipoli*

handbook and maps, or even just engrossed in a conversation, the warnings can be missed. Likewise, there are warnings of elk. These lumbering creatures have a penchant for the roads, and a collision with one is often fatal to both driver and beast. In northern Finland of course, the main hazard is reindeer—by the herd—and their colouring makes it very difficult to spot them. If you hit a reindeer you must inform the police. If you can bring yourself to do it, you should also cut off the dead animal's ear showing its owner's marking, and hand it in. This enables the owner to claim compensation, a most vital happening, for as I have stated elsewhere in this book, reindeer are still the lifeblood of Lapland's nomad people. Two final words on motoring in Finland. It is *not* allowed to lend your car to a Finn to drive, except where such activities are covered by schemes such as the one which will transport your vehicle for collection at journey's end. In other words no unofficial borrowing or loaning. And remember most of all that it is not allowed to drink *at all* when driving, not even one teeny one. Penalties are particularly severe, and will land you in jail without the option. Among all my many friends in Finland, most of whom love a party and any excuse for conviviality, I know nobody who will risk driving after even one drink. 'Better take a taxi' they say, so, when in Finland, follow their example.

3. Keski Suomi—the Central Province

A Finnish friend said to me one day, almost apologetically, yet with the sparkle in his eye that I have come to recognise as the hallmark of a humorous comment, though his face stays quite serious and virtually impassive, 'You know, we have over sixty thousand lakes really. The Swedes claim that they have over one hundred thousand, but I think it must have been raining when they counted them!'

It might be said with some justification that the Finns do get a bit fed up with the 'Land of a Thousand Lakes' tag, but there is no doubt that, apart from Helsinki and Lapland, there is one district which attracts more visitors from overseas than any other, and that is the Lake District of central Finland. By this, I mean the vast area stretching from Lahti to Jyvaskyla, from Tampere to Savonlinna. I make the distinction between overseas visitors and local holidaymakers, because the Finns themselves have such an affinity for the lakes and a very great majority have a cabin, or at least have access to a cabin in this area in which to take their summer holidays. (The rest seem to trot off to the southern archipelagoes in summer and Lapland in winter if they can.)

The lakelands, which form the very heart of Finland, were for centuries the main arteries, carrying all kinds of goods from one part of the country to another. Now, with efficient rail systems and good highways which also include bridges to many islands which were formerly isolated, steamers are no longer quite so vital to the welfare of the people in these erstwhile remote areas, and they have become almost entirely the province of the holidaymakers and the tourists, apart perhaps from the elderly man in his forester's cap and blue jersey, or an old lady with a black headkerchief, who prefer to stick to their long known ways and travel in more leisurely style. And, once having travelled with them, who can really say that they are so wrong? It is we with our passion for getting everything attended to within the shortest possible time, who are making the mistake of forgetting the gentler and more worthwhile aspects of living. Yet, on the lakes, one sees the evidences of today's living too . . . the great log rafts, shepherded by one minute, incredibly tough little tug, swimming down to the wharves at Valkeakoski or Viiala, and the chimneys of industrial Finland sometimes stand tall beyond the timberstacks of the blue-green forests and the browns, yellows and reds of the farmlands, so that one knows that still, the old and the new are inextricably mixed.

I took the road from Helsinki to Lahti early one very warm June morning some years ago, and, once out of the environs of the still sleepy city, the road stretched emptily, shimmering in the heat haze. There is a great deal of pleasure in motoring in Finland, just because one can see for a long way, and therefore one is able to take in so much more of all around than just the white line in the road and the lines marking the edges of the road and the beginning of the 'shoulders'. Already the yellowing grasses were stacked on the pikes to form the battalions of beehives which march in formation across the fields and the warm sunlight brought out the heavy scent of the pine and fir forests between which the road and the fields were wedged. I saw the sign to Jarvenpaa where Sibelius, that greatest of all Finnish composers, spent so much of his life, and where he is buried in his garden, but tempting as it was I didn't make the diversion. On through the neat villages of Mantsale and Orinattila, and in no time it seems I had covered the sixty-seven miles from Helsinki and was coming into the suburbs of Lahti.

Lahti means 'bay' in Finnish, and the town is situated on a small inlet beside Lake Vesijarvi, part of the lake district of Paijanne. I knew it was a fairly large city, with a population of about ninety thousand, but I was unprepared for the modernity of its buildings. Nothing seemed to remain of the past at all. The main reason for this was the terrible fire which completely destroyed the village of Lahti in 1877, and the new Lahti was started again on the ancient glacial ridge of Saila-pusselka, in 1905. One of the first of the modern buildings was the Town Hall, built in 1912 from a design by Eliel Saarinen, forerunner of many of the startling innovations in Finnish designs since then, but this building looks positively archaic in comparison with the surprising architecture of for instance, Joutjarvi Church, or the bank building, designed by Viljo Rewell, or the powerful radio masts, or the Mustankallionmaki Water Tower with its sightseeing terrace and views over the almost flat landscape. I wasn't at all sure that I was going to like Lahti at first. It seemed alien—not a bit how I'd pictured a town in central Finland. It certainly looked prosperous, with its furniture and metal industries and its famous brewery (I'd already sampled some of the products from that). It looked so very American, not Finnish at all, and this impression was heightened when my guide from the tourist office, who incident-ally is one of the prettiest girls I've ever met, spoke pure American! She told me that she'd been living in the States for a year or two. But in true Finnish style, she set out to make my visit thoroughly interesting and enjoyable, and I would like to pay tribute to her efforts, for it was entirely due to her that I saw so much, and that Lahti has remained so clearly in my memory.

Lahti is already famous for its winter sports activities, held at the end of February or beginning of March, and possesses one of the best skijumps in Scandinavia. The town constantly hopes that it will provide the venue for a Winter Olympics. Certainly, with some extra preparation, they would have the facilities. But Lahti is more famous for the International Writers Reunions which are held near by at Mukkula. 1963 saw the first of these, and the sixth such activity took place in June 1973 when the theme was 'Why write fiction?', calling for discussions on the usefulness of imaginative writing as opposed to stark fact. With Finland's absorption in the written word, it occurs to me that no better place could be chosen for such a venue. Certainly imagination was well to the fore in the choice of venue—Midsummer by Lake Vesijarvi, which is a delightful fact for anyone to write about.

The Hydrofoil *Tehi* makes her way from Lahti along Lake Paijanne to Jyvaskyla and the journey takes three hours. For people in a hurry this is one of the best ways to cover a lot of territory in as short a time as possible, seeing Finland, as it must be seen at least once, from water level, for it is fun, and entirely in keeping with modern Finland and its surroundings at its points of departure and arrival. But me . . . I like the silence and gentler pace of the older methods of water transport.

The camping site at Mukkula is rather a pleasant one, set in the grounds of what was once a manor house, now used as a restaurant, cafeteria, etc., and the whole area is termed a 'Tourist Centre', so that all sorts of activities go on there in summer months—folk dance performances, tennis, rowing, etc., and in winter they have a Snow Sculpture Exhibition. I felt that my own family efforts at rather lopsided snowmen would have come off very badly there, and of course the joy is that the sculptures stay in all their glory for weeks and are not, like the beautiful creations one used to see on the summer sands at British seasides, swept away by weather or tide changes. In summer the snow sculptures change places with an art exhibition, so there is always something to see at Mukkula of one sort or another.

There are a number of good hotels in Lahti in many price ranges, including Seurahuone, Musta Kissa, and Mukkula Summer Hotel, and lots of restaurants from the Quicksnack variety to the grander sort. I usually look for the places where one finds the locals; it seldom fails in any country. The place I enjoyed most was the Messilä Holiday Centre at Tirismaa, some five miles from Lahti, right on the shores of the sun-warmed lake. The estate dates back to the seventeenth century, but the manor house, which was completed in its present form in 1910, now serves as the restaurant, with a nostalgic atmosphere, and as a picture gallery. An exhibition was on when I was there. It was interesting, original and, to my inexperienced eye, some of the paintings were beautiful enough to live with. The main hotel is new, and very cleverly situated against a background of dark trees. The whole of the front of the building is glass, so that as one looks towards it it is almost indistinguishable from the trees, for only reflections of the leaves are visible. Inside, the hotel is as modern as tomorrow, with conference facilities, pleasant rooms, a large self-service café, two saunas, and two swimming pools as well. There are stables in the grounds, and decent-looking horses occupying them, mostly, I was told at the time I was there, of the Russian breeds, but that may have changed with new stock. There's fishing in summer and ice fishing in winter, delightful walks in the estate, and of course skiing on the trails in winter, and something that appealed to me immensely was that there was a special little play house for children, which reminded me of Hansel and Gretel. There is a small camping site in the grounds, without much in the way of facilities, but one could live in a tent or caravan and enjoy the other pleasantnesses by paying for them.

My road from Lahti took me straight through the heart of the lake country, across great bridges spanning the calm blue waters rippled only by the wake of a rowing boat, over islands, past red-painted farms and fields beside the reedy shores, where small boats lay half hidden awaiting their evening fishing excursions. The road surface wasn't all that it might have been —summertime is, after all, the only time when repairs can be carried out on Finnish roads and my summers couldn't be an exception, so one plunges on over rough patches and through the inevitable duststorms. But one delightful feature of these Finnish highways are the laybys. Marked well ahead, these are almost always deserted, with plenty of room to picnic, usually beside the lake, and sometimes even equipped with folding chairs and tables as well as log tables and benches; nobody bothers to remove them. Rather pleasant. There is seldom another person in sight, so one can take advantage of the little flight of wooden or stone steps leading down into the water to swim, and it is unbelievably warm. The comment that I enjoy swimming in Finland in summer is usually sufficient to make my hearers look at me as if I'm slightly off my rocker. Provided I can make them realise that Finland can be very warm in summer on occasion (for no-one ever believes statistics these days), it is quite simple. One look at the map contours shows that Finland's hills are very low, and it follows that her lakes too are shallow and therefore easily warmed by the summer sun, which shines for the best part of the twenty-four hours. The waters are much warmer than one would think, and are crystal clean into the bargain. When travelling in Finland, it is very tempting on a hot day to tarry awhile, to eat one's picnic by the water's edge and forget about the formidable list of appointments. After all, one argues with one's better self, this is holiday country isn't it, and how can one write about it if one rushes through? Sometimes the imp wins, and at others, one forces onwards . . . I stopped off just to have a quick look at Heinola one day, another spotlessly clean surprisingly wide-streeted little town, beside the Jurako Straits. Heinola was the capital of the province of Kymenkartano for a while, but its brief period of glory ended in 1843 when Mikkeli took over the job, and nowadays it lives on happily as a growing industrial town with a high reputation for its impressive Rheumatic Foundation Hospital, born as the result of its reputation as a former spa resort. It also has a nice camping ground at Heinäsaari, very easily found by turning left after crossing the bridge into the town, on to Kauppakatu (*katu* is a useful word to remember, for it means 'street'). Partly due to the very real risk of fire, and due to the desire in these days for preservation and conservation, the tendency is to persuade campers and caravanners to use the areas laid out for them, and certainly this is no hardship in Finland. I have seldom found better or cleaner sites anywhere. They range from the highly sophisticated, with every modern requirement of service shops, games rooms, good access roads, rowing boats, miniature golf, and holiday chalets, to the tiny site tucked away in the middle of a forest and reached over a bumpy cart track, but nearly always there is a sauna beside the lake. There are over three hundred sites spread over the entire country, and the majority are very clearly signposted from the main roads. From my own experience I would say that this is a good country for the caravanner, because there aren't so many hills to flog up and down, so that towing is easy. The number of caravans in Finland is growing, and there is a very lively Finnish Caravan Club, which holds rallies and always welcomes visitors from abroad. Details of both camping and caravanning possibilities are covered comprehensively in the many brochures available from the Finnish Tourist Board Offices, or direct from the Finnish Travel Association's Camping Department at Uudenmaankatu 16, Helsinki.

There is a very pleasant little camping site right beside the Oravakivensalmi Bridge at the provincial boundary line at Joutsa. This town likes to call itself the Gateway to Central Finland, maybe because the parish lies between the provinces of Hame and Savo. Anyway it is as good a place as any to start and there are two large maps by the road to help you not to lose yourself and at the far end of the bridge there is a small *kahvila* or café where the coffee is good. (One soon gets used to the Finnish signs—*kahvila* for café, *ravintola* for restaurant and *baari* for bar, although that doesn't necessarily mean they'll sell you a beer.) But I wasn't looking for any of these. I was heading for Joutsenlampi, one of the most famous holiday villages in Finland.

Holiday villages have become one of the most popular features of tourist Finland in the past few years, and offer a marvellous way of enjoying the peace of the Finnish countryside at reasonable cost. Most Finns go to their holiday cabins at every opportunity and these holiday villages are the nearest thing you can get to these unless you are lucky enough to have Finnish friends with their own precious hideaway. And in that case you are only reading this book for the sake of nostalgia! Most of the two hundred or so holiday villages are situated in the central lakeland area, but there are also some along the coasts, on the offshore islands and a few in the northern and eastern areas. They, like the camping sites, vary considerably, from a handful of cottages to as many as thirty-five, and from the simply but adequately furnished cabin variety to luxuriously equipped several-roomed apartments with their own garages, TV, fridges, etc. But nearly all of them, small or large, have their own little bit of beach and a rowing boat, and all offer a degree of privacy found in few places these days. More of the villages are beginning to offer programmed holidays, which include boating and fishing expeditions, barbecues on the shore, rambles, riding, water-skiing, tennis and so forth. And sauna naturally. But if you don't even want any of these simple pleasures, the choice is entirely your own. None of these holiday villages can be compared with holiday camps as we have come to think of them in Britain because they just wouldn't fit in with the Finnish way of life. It is an entirely different world, and I for one hope it stays that way.

By the time I reached the centre of Joutsa in late afternoon, in my obviously foreign Mini, I still hadn't seen any sign pointing to Joutsenlampi, and the Swedish road signs had petered out at the last roadworks. I went through the town and out on the far side, where the countryside slumbered into infinity, then back again along the main road, and after several more circuits and bumps of the small town, stopped beside an ice-cream kiosk in the main street to ask my way. I tried Swedish. The white-coated middle aged lady smiled, and shook her head. I tried German. She still smiled and shook her head. So I tried writing Joutsenlampi down. She looked at it, puzzled a minute, wrinkling her brow like a Disney spaniel, then made signs that I should wait. She came out of her kiosk, leaving it and the till wide open and clutching the bit of paper, trotted off down the street to where four of her erstwhile customers were sitting peaceably in a car, eating her wares. A conversation and a bit of arm waving, and then she trotted back again still smiling. The car with its cornet-eating occupants followed and drew up beside me. They all then indicated that I should get into my car and follow them. So, farewell and thanks to my stout benefactress, and off in minor procession. Obviously can't be far, thought I, but off we plunged, back on to the main highway and into the infinity that I had spurned, with the car's occupants nodding and smiling encouragingly from their rear window. Off down a country lane and hey presto!—Joutsen-lampi. The gates were ahead. We all stopped, shook hands all round and I repeated my two words of Finnish over and over again—*Kiitos* . . . *Näkemiin* (thank you, goodbye)—and they all bumped back along the lane, like the leprechauns, never to be seen again. Don't tell me that there aren't such things as good fairies. I met them in the countryside of central Finland.

From that moment I loved Joutsenlampi, and wherever I've stayed since, apart from special loves in Lapland, it has been one of my favourite places. Owned by the vast Rantasipi Hotel Group, the complex contains a large, extremely comfortable hotel, with rooms which opened on to small verandahs into the deep summer forest. The holiday village accommodation which I had come to see comprises very pleasant, beautifully designed and decorated bungalows, each with its own garage, set along the silver sand beside the huge expanse of lake; each has its private beach, together with a personal rowing boat. The sauna building is only a few yards away along the shore, and of course all the considerable facilities of the hotel itself, res-taurants, bars, discos, tennis courts, etc., as well as the lovely forest walks, are at everyone's disposal.

Most of the guests seemed to be German—quiet, middle-aged people seeking the same peaceful atmosphere that I was enjoying so much, but when I walked into the main lounge later that sunlit evening to watch the news bulletin on TV, I found a young English couple in sole occupancy. We had a drink together and started to exchange adventures. I discovered that they had taken a two-week package motoring tour, arranged from England with a well-known company specialising in Scandinavia, and had driven across Sweden to Turku and thence to the Lake District. All their accommodation had been arranged for them so that all they had to do was to drive and arrive in their small open sports car, and they had been, as I had, most impressed with the standards everywhere. Their main grumble was lack of time within Finland itself, rather than on the way to it, and it was brought home to me yet again that really one does need a three-week period if boats and one's own car are to be used. Only with fly/drive do you really get enough 'Finnish time' in a brief two weeks if you want to see Finland. If you are happy with including the other lovely countries as part of the trip, then the two-week driving package is to be highly recommended—it is all a matter of requirements and taste.

They had come on a different route and we compared notes. Their roads had been pretty hair-raising with, in one or two spots, surfaces which just didn't exist. But when I looked at their route I saw it had been on secondary roads which took them directly to ferries across the lakes to save time. Since then I've been back to look at those roads and they have, I'm happy to say, improved slightly. But country roads are country roads in central Finland and should be respected as such by any intending visitor.

I walked in the forest in broad daylight, at midnight and down to the lakeside. There was utter silence, and far out on the waters, a lonely little rowing boat sat, like a Japanese print, in silhouette against the rosy sunset of the sky. I left the doors wide open to the sweet scent of the forest and slept like a baby until awakened by the dive-bombing antics of a mosquito intent on his nightly feast. The mosquito screens weren't there for fun obviously, but I put the sheet over my head and he went away. British blood didn't appeal.

The placid lake waters felt like cool milk when I slipped in for a pre-breakfast swim on yet another perfect morning and I had the entire lake to myself. Even the rowing boat on the horizon had disappeared like a mirage. But as I strolled up to the main hotel building to help myself from the excellent and ample breakfast table, people were beginning to appear in bathing wraps of varied hues and sizes. I thought smugly that I'd had the best of it. Owner of a lake, just for a very little while, it was worth the effort . . . but paradise only lasts for just so long wherever it may be and all too soon I was back on the road heading for Jyvaskyla.

By virtue of its position at the head of Lakes Paijanne and

Jyvasjarvi, and almost in the middle of central Finland, Jyvaskyla has been a natural meeting place for centuries, mainly as a market place, but it became a town with its own charter in 1837 under the guidance of a Major Rosenbrojer, and since that time it has gone from strength to strength. It is now chief town of the district and has grown enormously in size with a population of over 56,000, many of them employed in the heavy industries of woodpulp processing and metal. But its main claim to fame surely must be its very important role in the educational processes of Finland, for it was here that teaching in the Finnish language started and the Jyvaskyla Compulsory Schoolteachers Training College began over a century ago, in 1863. The name changed to the Institute of Pedagogy in 1934, but with the setting up of an additional Arts Faculty in 1958 it became a university, and now it has the Teacher Training Department, thirty-one professorships and over four thousand students. Even more famous is the Summer University, started in 1912 as part of the Jyvaskyla University and drawing students from far beyond Finland's boundaries.

Naturally such a vital part of Finnish life could not be permitted to be carried on in anything but purely Finnish architecture, and who better to have created their highly individualistic styles than Professor Alvar Aalto. Indeed, if ever a town could be called 'his' town, this must be it, for apart from the very impressive practical and spacious university buildings (though like everywhere else they are now grumbling that they are too small) there is the Museum of Central Finland, with its magnificent art gallery, and Cygnaeus Park, with Saynatsalo Civic Centre, all products of Aalto's considerable talents. I suppose that in my rather hidebound English way I had been expecting something more on the lines of our older universities when I went to visit Jyvaskyla, and although I had looked at a picture or two beforehand I was completely unprepared for the brick buildings which confronted me. 'Redbrick' took on a new dimension. Until then it had always signified Victorian and Edwardian architecture at its very worst. But this was beautiful, flowing, dignified and completely in character with the countryside around it. For me that is one of the great facets of Aalto's genius. He seems to identify everything he builds with Finland's natural contours and yet, of course, his styles have changed dramatically over the years, modifying and adapting to Finnish needs at the time of each design or building as well as to his own artistic growth. The University staircase and hall impressed me particularly because it gives a feeling that it is 'outside and inside all at once'. Again implying that education is part of a nation and not just tucked away inside a building to be let out now and then. Saynatsalo on the other hand is much smaller than I had thought from photographs, but it does look like the centre of a community and that after all is what it is. When one compares it with the 'workers' building' built by Aalto in 1925, still in Jyvaskyla . . . blank walls and functional designs . . . is it the community which has grown in stature or Aalto? Or both?

My visit to Jyvaskyla coincided with three important things: a heatwave, the annual arts festival, and a visit to the university and festival by the Prime Minister. The first was dealt with by having a cool salad lunch at the top of the lookout tower, but the second and third got a bit mixed up. My Finnish friend, a large-boned lady who is exactly as one imagines the women of central Finland should be—seemingly serious, exceedingly courteous, and obviously strong—had somehow squeezed herself into the Mini with me and we drove in fine style to the front door of the university to find a suspicious absence of cars and everybody on best behaviour. My dirty little car stopped. People rushed forward, looked a bit alarmed and it was hastily explained that at any moment the Great Man was due to arrive, so we changed plans and drove off to visit the museum first instead of going to hear one of the seminar sessions of the Arts Festival. Far be it from me to upset long and carefully laid preparations. But we spent longer in the gallery than we'd intended. It is a beautiful building inside, but I must admit that I'd been hard put to it to understand most of the items on display and made no comments, apart from the appropriate noises. My friend looked hard at me. 'Tell me,'

she said in her careful English, 'Do you understand any of
them?' I had to be honest. 'NO.' She came as near to a giggle
as her stately bearing would allow. 'Neither do I,' she said,
'But I had to bring you to see them for yourself.' We were
laughing uncontrollably, quite alone in the museum, at ourselves not at the exhibits, for trying to be something we were
not, when there was an influx of visitors, all extremely solid
citizens, obviously all dignitaries of sorts. We sobered our faces
as best we could, the leading gentleman said, 'Good afternoon,'
and we chorused our replies in English and Finnish and
scuttled down the corridor and out into the sunshine. 'That,'
said my companion as we reached the safety of the Mini, still
laughing, 'was the Prime Minister. I hope he understood it all
better than we,' but how could he possibly understand that he
had met a mad Englishwoman in a museum unless someone
explained it to him? Art surely isn't something to laugh at—or
with.

We went back to the University, where we could now park
where we liked, and spent some time in the packed auditorium,
listening to a thesis, but once the thread has gone, it is impossible to pick it up again, so I contented myself with looking at
the rapt faces of the international audience. The arts festival
at Jyvaskyla has become one of the highlights of the Finnish
summer scene, and represents culture at its most varied.
Seminars, congresses . . . each year has a different theme. Our
year was environmental; there were extra-mural lectures, music,
exhibitions, jazz, theatre groups, excursions, recitals, modern
and folk dancing, and in the evenings, when Finland always
wakes up, cafés, restaurants and bars were filled to overflowing
and a great time seemed to be had by all. I envied them a little,
just a little, and wished I was twenty years younger, just for the
ability to think as they were thinking and understand it all a
bit better—but only if I could have taken the twenty years'
wisdom or folly back with me! Otherwise the second chance
would come out exactly as the first. It always has a habit of
doing so, I find.

Soon I was headed southwards again via Korpilahti and

Jamsa, crossing from mighty Lake Paijanne past endless little lakes and farmsteads in pleasant, relaxed but unexciting country, to Tampere, placed on its isthmus between the Nasijarvi and Pyhajarvi lakes. This area is the most western part of Finland's lake district. Tampere, or Tammerfors, was given its charter by Gustavus III, King of Sweden in 1779, but already the town had become the natural meeting place for people of the district because of its accessibility by land and water, and industry began to spring up along the banks of the Tammerkoski rapids, known sometimes as the Mother of Tampere. It was the first town in Finland to have electric light. The first aircraft flight in Finland took place there. Nowadays it is known worldwide for its textiles. This industry was started by a Scotsman, James Finlayson, who had been working in Russia as an engineer, and after a visit to Finland set up a small business in Tampere in 1820, eventually establishing a spinning mill which imported the cotton from England with which to work. At that time many of the inhabitants of the district lived in the small wooden houses at Pispala (some of the houses still exist and are used in the folk festivals); they were fairly healthy folk because of their country upbringing, but Finlayson rejected many of them because he thought they wouldn't be strong enough if they were small, as most were, and only took the bigger people. This, I suppose, must have been a hangover from his own remembrances of industrial England, where undersized people went hand in hand with undernourishment and an inability to work hard. Quite a few Britons joined him in the community there, and the small cemetery bears witness to many who ended their days in faraway Finland. Finlayson sold out some years later, but the firm is still known as Finlayson–Forssa and today one sees many items with this label in the British markets, along with many other brand names from Tampere, which between them have succeeded in making the city the second largest and most prosperous in Finland. It has been described as Finland's Manchester, but this is exceedingly unfair on Tampere, because it is a much pleasanter, prettier place in spite of its vast industrial potential. Much of that is carefully tucked away and doesn't obtrude quite so much—yet. Neither does it conflict with the impression that Tampere is still very much a city in the wilderness—yet.

Perhaps the best place to start to look at what Tampere can show its visitors is where it all began: on Pyynikki Ridge. Now a park area this was the cliff beside the great sea of Yoldia after the Glacier Period, and must be at least ten thousand years old. The bedrock formation is particularly interesting to geologists for it is thought to be among the most ancient in the world. Nowadays the ridge, roughly about 450 feet high, is covered by aged pine trees and is a particularly pleasant place on which to walk, affording intriguing glimpses of the lake through the trees. There is also an observation tower which affords a better view. There is another tower, the highest in Finland, called Näsinneula at Särkanniemmi on the other side of Tampere beside the planetarium. These towers are so much part of the Finnish landscape that I am inclined to forget them, yet their role is vital, for in such wooded countrysides as Sweden and Finland there is no other way in which to keep an eye for the dreaded fires which could destroy the 'Green Gold' of the forest so quickly and completely, and the magnificent views too, would be impossible to obtain elsewhere in this gently curved countryside.

Within the area of Pyynikki is the famous summer theatre. There are several of these open-air theatres in Finland, for in the long light evenings people are anxious to stay outside as long as possible. But Pyynikki is special: it was the first theatre in the world to have a revolving auditorium, for by means of a turntable the entire audience is moved to face another direction and another scene, without stirring a muscle of their own. One moment the scene may be against the backdrop of the greys, blues or silvers of the lake, the next against the long line of Pyynikki ridge, yet another the dark black and green of an evening forest. I arrived during rehearsal one day when chaos reigned, for they all seemed to be rehearsing in rather the same manner as for television or films, with no real cohesion in individual performances, all on the same minute stage, while

7   *Pyynikki open-air theatre*

unrequired performers sat on the grass, under the stages, or in the wooden seated auditorium. But when I went back that same evening, the magic of the theatre had woven its spell as I knew it must. Naturally the play was in Finnish, although there are commentaries in Swedish and other languages are used from time to time in the repertoires. But it lived—oh, how it lived. It was the dramatisation of Vaino Linna's *The Unknown Soldier*, still by far one of the most popular plays ever to be performed in Finland, and the bitternesses, the sorrows, the humours, the desperate and overriding honesty and the despair were all there, among the firing of the tanks and the acrid stage smoke blowing through the pine trees. I forgot the hard seats, the language difficulties, the chill in the evening air and even the efforts of the mosquitoes to gain attention. To try and understand Finland and the Finns perhaps it is essential to try to visit such a theatre and such a performance; it will still be a virtually impossible task in a short visit, but an unforgettable experience.

There are so many nice things in Tampere too, apart from its people. The four splendid figures on the Hameensilta bridge, carved by Waino Aaltonen, for instance, deserve more than a passing glance from the car, for they have a purpose, and a place in Finnish history. The statues personify the Pirkkalaiset, a Finnish-speaking tribe who were the people who collected the taxes and trade monopolies with the Lapps, touched upon elsewhere in this book. It has been assumed that the name came originally from the Kirkkala district, which is near Tampere, and so Aaltonen represented the four figures as symbols of Finnish pride, by making them a huntsman, a merchant, a tax collector and a beautiful woman. Aaltonen was always one of the most nationalistic of all Finnish sculptors, and one finds his work in many other places in Finland, but these, to me, *are* Aaltonen.

I rather like Tampere Cathedral too. A beautiful building in the old style, completed in 1907 when Finland was still a Grand Duchy under Russia, it has a feeling of Russia about it —a sadness too, indefinable, and yet there is enormous tenacity to life and faith in it when one gazes at the 'Resurrection' by

8   Lake Pyhäjärvi, Tampere

Magnus Enckell. But to me it is the frescoes along the balcony which are endearing and so very symbolic. They depict twelve naked boys, each bearing in his own way a portion of the thorny garland of life. At the time that Hugo Simberg painted this work it took all the powers of persuasion of many famous artists in Finland to persuade the incensed congregation that they indeed possessed a great work of art, for to make matters worse Simberg had placed a serpent in the roof vaultings. The work took two years and greatly affected Simberg's health. There are two other pieces of his work in the Cathedral too: 'The Wounded Angel', which is made beautiful by the two small boys who carry the drooping figure on a makeshift litter with such determination; I'm not so happy about the 'Garden of Death'. All Simberg's representations of death verge on the macabre, although they sometimes have a twisted humour too, and I was glad to turn back to the delicate figures of the boys and the garland.

If you are unlikely to get further east than Finland, it is worth having a look at the Eastern Orthodox church in Tampere, because it is the only one of its kind in Scandinavia, and, apart from the rich ornamentation, claims the biggest bells in Finland. I never heard them ring . . .

Of great interest to me, and I think to anyone who wants to see the more remarkable and unusual aspects of modern Finnish architecture, is a visit to Kaleva Church in Tampere. Even from a distance it is impressive, standing on its slight rise. It was designed by Reima Pettilä and Raili Paatelainen, and completed in 1966. When one looks at it closely, and from all angles, one realises that it is in the shape of a fish. After all, a fish was the symbol of the first Christians. Its great walls are solid pieces, soaring high above one's head, cathedral-like in their stark beauty, pure in their simplicity. The organ is very fine, and so too is the carved altarpiece, but it was the area below the church in the living rock which attracted me so much. All the activities which take place with a church as their nucleus can be held there in a series of rooms which can be extended or compressed as desired—even kitchens for the coffee and buns and weddings. I couldn't help feeling too, that this building could serve very well as a place of safety for a great many people in times of further troubles in Finland. May God forbid the terrible necessity, but remembering the terrors of bombardment both in Finland and elsewhere in Europe, one does not easily forget to look at places with a 'double eye'.

I suppose one should mention the planetarium. It is after all, the only one in Scandinavia, and is a magnificent achievement. It has very special projection facilities and covers the six thousand stars which can be seen by man. But then this city has endless varieties of educational material in abundance: the aquarium for instance, the gymnastic museum or the museum which houses a collection of relics from the province of Hame. And of course, the Lenin museum, which has so many mementoes of Lenin's stay in Finland. I remember being told by a friend of mine in Finland that he once saw Lenin, that at first sight he was unimpressive, but that 'there was something that made him apart from other people'. But it is the modernity of Tampere itself which to me is the most interesting. All the architecture isn't necessarily good, but it is at least a little different, and the streets are all wide, and that in itself is a great change for an industrial town of these dimensions. Finally, before you go from this city, find time to go and look at the ceramic tapestry by Birger Kaipainen. This mural was designed and made specially by him for the Montreal Exhibition of 1967 and is composed of multicoloured violets and elegant swans. It belongs to Tampere University and has pride of place there. Its Finnish name is 'Orvokki Meri', and it is exquisitely worked.

There are a number of reliable and comfortable hotels in Tampere, as well as some very good restaurants. I had an excellent beef stew for lunch one day in the Sorsapuiston Grilli, a *ravintola* with old Finnish atmosphere, although they also have a modern section. It is quite near the children's playground, and there is usually parking space near by. I had a marvellous evening once with a party of journalists from *Aamulehti*, the local Tampere newspaper, at Sillankorva. We ate, we danced, and we sang; the restaurant even supplied us with songbooks and I still treasure my copy. But one of our party had to stay on Coca-Cola and coffee, for we had to drive home and journalists can't spare the time for a jail sentence.

Another time I stayed at one of the excellent motels in the vicinity of Tampere. I chose Motorest Jäähovi Motel, but I could equally well have plumped for Harmala, about 5 kilometres from the centre of Tampere. Both are good; no frills, but efficient and, as always in Finland, spotlessly clean.

The large camping site at Harmala has a lot to recommend it too, and when I was there I was particularly taken with the excellent cooking facilities, all under 'open cover', which consist of rows of stoves, sinks etc., so that one need not go to all the fag of getting one's own cooker set up at the end of perhaps a long, tiring day's travelling—particularly welcome if it happens to be raining. There are a number of small log cabins at Harmala, but these get taken very early in the day, and often people hire them for longer periods. Again there were many nationalities at the site, the atmosphere was very friendly and of course—need I say it—swimming and sauna right at the lakeside. The beaches in this area are extremely popular because the water temperatures frequently reach 70° in midsummer and they can be a bit crowded, but by going a little further afield there is no problem.

There are three Silverline boat routes from Laukontori Harbour in Tampere. One goes north to Ruovesi through the Murole Canal, built in 1854, and to Kallela, the atelier of the painter Gallen-Kallela who portrayed so vividly and so forcefully all the strange tales of the Kallevalan motifs. They are known now outside Finland, but at the time that he was painting these heroic legends Gallen-Kallela was also building this rather imaginative studio, when romanticism in architecture was very new in Finland. Hugo Simberg, whose work I have commented upon in Tampere Cathedral, was a pupil of Kallela, and the cliff paintings which you see en route to the studio by the Silverline are attributed to both him and Kallela. The boat eventually ties up at Ruovesi, a nice little town with a small wooden church, but it is mainly famous for the fact that the greatest of Finland's national poets, Runeberg, spent two summers here at Petoniemi Mansion, and wrote much work there, and it was from that time that this part of the lake route got the title, 'The Poet's Way'.

Inevitably came the morning when I arrived at the Laukon-tori harbour to catch the boat for the 7-hour trip down to Aulanko. I gave my car keys to the office, for it was arranged that the car would be driven down to await my arrival at the other end. This is an excellent facility which is available on many lake routes within Finland and it does enable the driver to take a rest from the wheel. I went on board. It was a dear little boat, with rows of benches on the upper deck and a large cabin with plenty of window space to take advantage of the views as one eats. These steamers are rather reminiscent in a way of the Thames steamers, only there aren't any noisy accordions— at least, there weren't on mine. Apart from the fact that there are so many small summer cabins beside the waters (where all Finns love to hide themselves from Fridays to Mondays and for a month at a time in the summer), this lake area is very different to the waters of Saimaa and Paijanne, for it goes through some of the most interesting countryside of Finland from the historian's point of view, for the Swedish influences here were very strong. But little of anything is apparent except the waters and the forests for the first two hours or so on board from Tampere and one drifts along in a pleasant daze, relaxing completely to the gentle insistence of the engines and the slight movement of the boat. Small islands loom up. There's usually a small cottage and a sauna, and someone fishing or just sitting or pottering happily on his rock. We stopped at a couple of small piers in the middle of nowhere to let people on and off, slipping away with a brief salute on the ship's hooter, and then it began to rain. It blotted everything from sight, driving us before the storm, and forcing even the hardiest among us to take refuge in the saloon. But it was wonderful too, because, out of the gloom came the real indication that this is indeed part of the vital communications system of Finland. A small

tug, pushing forward into the rains, which had become tropic-
ally heavy and roughened the waters, was towing endless
numbers of log rafts behind her, while men moved from raft to
raft in the time-honoured, log-jumping way, making it all look
so easy. There must have been at least a hundred thousand logs
in some of the loads. Much of the timber of Finland is carried
on the lakes in summertime, but in winter the lakes are completely frozen and buses and snowploughs take over as the lakeland's transport to the islands. It is often easier to visit one's
neighbours in the lakeland provinces in winter by skiing across
the ice than in summer. The days before the advent of motor
boats must have been quite interesting, for to get to church
there were special 'church boats' and there is a mention of
these in a handbook for travellers, written I believe by a John
Murray in 1849, where it is said that they were 'pulled by about
twenty women, while an equal number of men smoked their
pipes in the stern'. I am indebted to Mr Mead for unearthing
that contribution to the flames of Women's Lib!

At Viiala one passes the wood-processing factories and from
thereon the waterway is extremely narrow. Even though the
boat moves very slowly the reeds bow low in the high wash. By
the time we reached this point the rain had stopped, so the
human cargo of the Silverline boat were in full cry on deck
again, but the skies were still grey and the contrast to the
heat of the previous days was very marked. I was glad of a
heavy woollen blazer jacket, so it is wise to be prepared for any
eventuality in Finland's weather.

At Viidennumero (that means 'number five' in English)
there is a magnificent suspension bridge, and a tourist restaurant
by the lakeside with plenty of parking space. From here one
can take the other branch route along the lake towards Kanga-
sala and Kaivanto. This is perhaps the prettiest route of all,
because one passes old stone churches from the fifteenth and
eighteenth centuries, bridges, ancient hill ridges like the
Pyynikki one, Valkeakoski, a busy, highly modern town where
the houses tend to be more like our own in that they are houses
rather than apartments, and one can visit the villa and the

studio of Emil Wikstrom, one of Finland's famous sculptor sons, at Visavuori. There is hardly a tour of this part of Finland which doesn't visit this studio, so it can be busy in summer. At least his work looked naturalistic, and therefore, one presumes, life-like. But from Viidennumero on this trip I was pointed towards Hameenlinna, Aulanko and Hattula. Hameenlinna itself is a smallish town, unremarkable in its architecture, more reminiscent of old-fashioned Swedish towns than the modernity of so many of Finland's urban areas. But it has one great claim to fame. It was the birthplace of Jean Sibelius, whose genius for so perfectly expressing his country in music makes one want to cry. His old home on Halligukatu is open to the public, but I must admit that every single time I have been in Hameenlinna I have found it closed for some reason or another. So I content myself with the memorial in Helsinki and find consolation in a concert in Finlandia Hall.

The old castle at Hameenlinna is worth a quick look, mainly for its age and the fact that it exists at all. So little remains in Finland from the Middle Ages that it is worth hanging on to the bits that do. Eventually it is hoped that the castle will be restored as Turku Castle has been, but this is a very costly business for a country with so many demands on its slender resources. Hattula Church, dating from the same period and about five miles distant from Hameenlinna, is worth visiting, if only for its painted threats of Hellfire and Damnation and for its very beautiful pulpit. Notice too that it is brick built. This would have been a very expensive undertaking in the fourteenth century in this wild country, so it must have been very important to the good folk of Hame. Near by there is an old farmyard and a museum with typical Hame relics from by-gone ages. Remember that this was one of the most powerful provices of all Finland, one of the most wealthy and supposedly also the most stubborn. Not quite so pleasant, but equally important in Finnish history is the Tank Museum at Parola, and the Tank Memorial in the garrison grounds.

I have an affinity for graveyards, if they are old enough. There is an extremely ancient one at Myllymaki, with finds from about 500 B.C. There is one grave, supposedly of a soldier, which dates from about nine hundred years ago. Who was he I wonder? How came he thence? Question and answer only receive silence in the summer Finnish landscape, but it crosses my mind that here is a mystery; it reminds me, without any cogent reason, of the Rufus Stone in our own New Forest. So long ago . . . So long? It is but yesterday in Nature.

Today's people are on holiday at busy Aulanko. One sees them as the boat pulls in at the pier. Swimming, playing tennis, golfing, fishing, water-skiing or lazing. This is one of the grand hotels of Finland, although these days it is being extended so much that it has lost a lot of its old elegantly leisured style. I remember on my first visit, when I was taken around by a pretty little Finnish hostess of about nineteen summers—nearly all the hostesses I ever meet in Finland seem to be little and pretty and very young: I suppose they all settle down after all this escorting of foreigners!—and as we creaked upwards in an elderly lift whose doors had to be manually operated she said apologetically, 'I am afraid I must show you another part of the building now. You will excuse it please. It is very old.' 'How old?' I asked idly, expecting a couple of hundred years at least. '1925,' she said, and I felt like Methuselah!

Aulanko is a very comfortable place in which to stay. Built originally by an exceedingly wealthy man, Colonel Hugo Standerskjold, for his own use, the house must have been very beautiful as a private home in its heyday. No expense was spared. The colonel built long roads, artificial lakes, summer-houses, a viewing tower, even a castle ruin, and then placed statues along the lakeside. Now it has everything that a modern holiday complex could require. Restaurant, bars, nightclub, conference rooms, beautiful swimming pool and sauna, hair-dressers, shops and all the other impedimenta which seem to be inseparable from luxury holidays. I've stayed there several times now. The place always seems to be full of 'special anniversaries' of some sort or another. Elegantly coiffured and dressed ladies with their immaculate escorts in the rather prim evening Finnish style which suits them so well, and yet which is very similar to the upper class Swedish manner which some Finns affect to dislike. The long speeches and the toasts, the dancing, the inevitable chatter which goes on in all the powder rooms all over the world . . . I like Aulanko in all seasons, but I think I enjoyed it best when it was heavy snow outside, and the warm lobbies sucked in a breath of ice along with the fur-coated guests. I enjoy watching the manners and modes in all countries, particularly in Scandinavia. It always takes an hour or two for the first formalities to wear off, but then one sees the fur fly just that little bit faster!

The road back to Helsinki is uneventful, busier than many others in Finland because it is a main one, but by our standards one would think everyone had gone to the moon. Particularly in winter, when it is a grey road rather than white, enlivened only by small towns or the passing wheeze and splashing of a lorry. In summer it is rather pleasanter. There is one place which is rather nice to visit, and that is the Glass Museum at Riihimäki. This town is about 37 kilometres from Hämeenlinna, and about 66 kilometres from Helsinki. The town is the headquarters of Riihimäki Oy, one of the famous glassworks of Finland, (founded there in 1910) by which time the town had already become a crossroads for the railway system which also helped its prosperity. Glass and glassblowers came to Finland from Germany and Sweden, first only to put windowpanes into the new-fangled window spaces, and then later to make glass objects, and the industry has grown to enormous proportions since the first glassworks was founded at Uusikaupunki in 1681. The museum, which has some rather special pieces, wasn't too difficult to find, although it is tucked away in a side street up a small hill (most unusual feature in this part of Finland) and I went through a large stone archway to find myself in what appeared to be the driveway of a very pleasant old house. At my knock the door was opened by a gentleman who turned out to be the curator in person. I started to apologise for my late call, but he brushed it aside, saying that the apology should come from him as his daughter was practising on the piano! And indeed, faintly through the wooden walls came the oh so familiar sounds of a struggling little performer. It was rather the right atmosphere and accompaniment for glass, a fragile yet immensely strong substance which takes time and patience to perfect.

There are several items from the beginnings of the Finnish glassworks era, in the Riihimäki collection, but the museum doesn't only concentrate on Finnish glass. There are some pieces there which are as much as two thousand years old; others came but yesterday. Bottles, old household items, vases in lead crystal, tools used in the industry for generations, books on every facet of making glass, but, most beautiful of all, the magnificent and unique items which have set the patterns and the standards of the fame of Finnish glass right across the globe. In spite of their priceless value, I just couldn't have lived with some of them, but there were one or two examples of the art of Riihimäki's own special artist, Gunnel Nyman, who worked with the firm until her early death in 1947. She had worked with other glassworks too, but her name is still associated with the Riihimäki work. Her speciality was to combine opaline and clear crystal and to place designs one inside the other . . . exquisite reflections of pure light. But she also designed some excellent everyday stuff, and this is still popular. There are many specimens of other works too in this Museum, from Iittala, and Johannisland, Nuutajärvi, and from many famous design names in the industry, Wirkkala, Franck, Sarpaneva, Nanny Still and Alvar Aalto—yes, he works in glass too!—and my splendid curator knew every piece personally. Before I left, he excused himself for a moment, and returned, bearing a book in one hand, and a small glass paperweight in the other. 'These,' he said, 'are to remind you of us.' The paperweight is circular and flat and has the shape of a bottle impressed in it (after all, the first glass was in bottle shapes) and the name of the works, written in Finnish and English. The book, full of pictures of Riihimäki's progress and prowess as a town, has the inscription 'Many thanks for your visit to our museum', the date and Mr Pentinnen's signature. Thanks for coming . . . It was I who required to thank him.

Try to call in at Riihimäki when you are on the road to the lakes of central Finland, or on the way back from them. Glass, like water, belongs in the countryside of this green, blue and white landscape.

4. Lapland

Why is it that certain place-names are so evocative? It may be in some instances because a story heard or a picture seen in childhood becomes engrained in the memory, so that the mere mention of that name is enough to set the imagination alight and the heart pounding. Sadly, all too often, when the ambition to visit the longed-for Shangri-la is fulfilled the reality is disappointing, for dreams so seldom come true in this old world of ours.

I think I have been luckier in some respects. For many years I longed to visit Lapland, but my path led in other directions, so that it has only been in comparatively recent times that I was able to see the 'top of Europe', and I was not disappointed. On the contrary, it was exactly as I had imagined it to be, and much more. For me there was a peace, a tranquillity, that I have never found in any other place: the loneliness, the immensity, the desolation, and the feeling that here at least one can forget the stupidity and triviality and the shallowness of so much of the trimmings of our civilisation for a little while. One cannot pretend in the savage face of Nature. It calls for a physical courage, and to a very great extent mental courage too, so that one is stripped at least to oneself of the façade which must be shown elsewhere. I have been back as often as I can, for the far north has its own built-in transmitter to those who are attuned to its very special frequency, and it calls, insistently, and loudly, to those with ears to hear.

Lapland is not confined to Finland. It embraces a huge area, stretching right across Norway, Sweden, Finland and into the u.s.s.r. It is the region where Lapps live and where the Lapp tongue is spoken. Incidentally, the Lapps never refer to themselves as 'Lapp', preferring 'Samek' or 'Saame', and this word is increasingly used by Norwegians and Swedes when referring to Lapps, in addition to the Norwegian use of 'Finner', not to be confused with the Swedish use of the same word meaning the Finnish people! In some ways it is impossible to separate one region of Lapland from another, for the life in Norway, Sweden and Finland at least, must, by the very nature of the terrain, be similar. But while Norwegian Lapland has a long, deeply indented coastline to the Arctic Ocean, Swedish Lapland has none, and since the setting up of new borders with the u.s.s.r. at the end of the 1941–44 war, confirmed by the Peace Treaty of Paris in 1947, neither has Finnish Lapland, and this does have a definite effect on the economies and general way of life, for of necessity each country has a different approach to the immense problems that living in these latitudes can bring.

Norway, quite naturally, depends on its northern waters for a great deal of its fishing industries as well as the highly valuable mineral deposits that can be forced from the fierce landscape; her coast Lapps (or sea Finns) also depended on fishing for part of their existence, though this was mostly for whale or seal, and nowadays they combine fishing and farming as they have become less nomadic in their habits. Sweden's great iron mines at Kiruna and Gallivare are the focal points for thriving industries, drawing workers from everywhere as well as some Lapps, but much of the rest of the vast tracts of land are protected as National Parks, and in addition only Swedes of Lapp descent, who hold the Lapp right, may breed reindeer, so that Swedish Lapps are known as forest or river Lapps, drawing much of their income and livelihood from farming, game and fish.

Finland lost one of her greatest riches when the nickel mines of Petsamo had to be ceded to Russia as part of the war reparations, and although there is still a small amount of copper and iron mining, there is very little industrial activity in Finnish Lapland, although the present efforts to harness the great power potential of the northern rivers to hydro-electric schemes could well change the picture considerably in the next few years. In Finland, Finns as well as Lapps are permitted to keep reindeer, and only about a quarter of the animals are in Lapp hands. There have been many attempts to improve reindeer farming, but much more research is needed and this is, as always, hampered to some extent by cost. Reindeer meat is very expensive, even when one buys it in the north, let alone in restaurants in other parts of Scandinavia, but how can it be otherwise when there is lack of grazing in certain areas—a problem that certainly could never have been envisaged even a few decades ago? The difficult, bare terrain, with its sparsely scattered communities has much to do with the lack of employment to be found in the north, but it is also due to a considerable extent to the 1941–44 war. Under the terms of the Armistice Treaty with Russia in 1944 the Finns had to turn on their erstwhile Nazi Allies and drive about two hundred thousand troops from Lapland. The same thing that had happened to North Norway happened in Finland. As they retreated, the Nazis destroyed everything—farms, villages, even cattlesheds and crops, so that after the holocaust the whole of Finnish Lapland was littered with the smoking ruins of a lifetime's work. It was a senseless destruction, but is war ever anything else? Almost immediately the Finns set to work, often with bare hands, to replace the loss, and within ten years so great was their effort that it was difficult to know where the destruction had been, except within the minds of the people who had witnessed it. This accounts for the fact that one can find little of the past in northern Finland, and indeed for the similarity of so many of the sparsely scattered smallholdings. This similarity is compensated for by the fact that the landscape itself is infinitely more varied.

There are fells and rivers, moors and lakes, which, by the time one reaches the imperceptible borders of Lapland have taken the place of the endless forests of the southern landscape. Most of the trees of the north are small, squat, often dwarf birch, bracing themselves firmly against the winds, the rain and the driving snow on the sides of the *tunturi*. Along the rivers and lakes one finds thin spruce, while weatherbeaten Norway pines make their homes on rocky knolls that would deter less-determined trees. But below one's feet, across the shoulders of those hills and over the moorland, or among the trees, there are small shrubs which, in the brief months of glorious summer, produce sweet blueberries and scented yellow cloudberry so that fingers and mouths are stained with the tell-tale juice. The elusive Arctic strawberry too, finds its home here, and in autumn, just before the winter comes, there are the last of the wild edible fungi. There is a perfume in the air in summer, thin, delicate, indefinable, yet unmistakably the scent of the north. Step down from a plane at Ivalo, or from the country bus after hours of travel from Rovaniemi, or just out from the snug warmth of a small hotel among the trees in the early morning, and one feels like a captive animal lifting its head to sniff at sweet freedom or like a prisoner suddenly, gloriously, free from his chains.

It is inevitable that if one approaches the Arctic Circle from the south of Finland one arrives at Rovaniemi, called euphemistically in the travel brochures, the 'Gateway to Finnish Lapland'. Rovaniemi is in fact situated just a fraction south of the Polar Circle, but the airport of the town is just above it. Rovaniemi didn't escape the destruction of 1944, and there are only a very few houses left in the whole town which date from before that time. When it was decided to rebuild, Alvan Aalto, among the greatest of all Finnish designers—perhaps among the greatest of contemporary world designers—was asked to formulate the town plan, and this was then executed by other well-known Finnish architects.

The town is entirely modern in conception, but Aalto decided to make the design in the form of a reindeer's antlers as befitted the municipal centre of an area which still depends greatly on this ubiquitous beast. The result is interesting and at least it avoids the straight up-and-down effect that one so often gets in new towns. But whenever I go there, I cannot shake off the feeling that this is a frontier town. Perhaps this is because so many of the streets have gravel surfaces which to urban eyes give a raw, unfinished look to the town. I have to keep reminding myself that for much of the year the gravel is hidden under snow and ice. But still the impression is with me, and I would never be surprised to see a door open and a Wild West cowboy, complete with stetson and gunbelt come hurtling out looking for his horse. There is a distinct link with the Wild West anyway, everywhere one goes in the north. On every bookstand, cowboy stories feature high in the popularity stakes among the paperbacks, and after all, the Lapps can be said to be the true cowboys of the north. One look at them, complete with lariat and all too often, bowed legs, and one ceases to wonder quite so hard why they are such avid readers about Deadwood Dick! And frontier town isn't so inaccurate a description in some ways because, with a population of nearly thirty thousand souls, Rovaniemi is the last big town in Finland on the long haul to the north. The three hundred miles on to the Norwegian border have small towns of varying sizes, but it is to Rovaniemi that the entire area looks as 'the capital'.

Certainly one can find practically anything one wants there, and womanlike I enjoy pottering around the little shops, or the larger drapery or grocery stores and supermarkets, because it always gives one a so much clearer idea of the way people live out their daily lives. A look in a ladies' outfitters is revealing. Most of the winter clothing is orientated towards padded three-quarter coats with matching trousers in waterproofed nylon material and nearly all of them in very bright colours. Because houses are of necessity very warm inside, dresses are lighter in weight than ours, many in the popular Marimekko designs which are now slowly finding their way on to many British dress-racks. But the ones found inside Finland are still, to my eyes, much bolder, even more garish. Yet Finnish women can look dazzling in them, probably because they are on the whole taller than us. In summer clothing too, accent is usually on lighter weights and lighter colours, but still in Rovaniemi the designs are on the dull side in comparison with the things to be found in Helsinki. Underclothing was downright boring, so too was footwear. But then, who could wear fashion shoes in a

9 The 'hat of the four winds', showing the streamers reserved for special occasions

10 A safari halts while skiers take a breather too; Lapland

frontier town anyway, and when the temperatures are *really* down, in winter, it is impossible to wear nylon stockings without a covering layer of thick longjohns. Nylons alone will stick to the skin and one removes it along with the stocking. In quite a different category are the winter boots and of course skiboots and sports equipment of all kinds—all of these can be a very good buy if one is selective.

There are naturally many souvenir shops in Rovaniemi, not a lot different from Helsinki in content and pricing, and if one is going further north it is worth waiting to buy things like reindeer skins and boots from the Lapp villages such as Enontekio, Inari or Ivalo, if only for the fact that you bought them from the hands of the owner himself. The paler skins are more expensive than the dark ones and far more difficult to obtain, but you can expect to pay upwards of £10 for a good size whole dark skin. *Soled* reindeer boots are a good buy for winter wear, and the fur-soled variety make splendid house-shoes providing one puts an inner sole in them (without inner soles the hand-sewn seams are very hard on the feet until they have softened down with use). But although they are completely warm and dry on the cold hard-packed dry snow of north Finland, where I have worn them for long periods, they cannot be worn outside in our damp English climate. The wet comes through the skin, though it dries very quickly. Since finding out the hard way, I have wondered if it is just the same when the skin is still on the reindeer! Interesting thought . . .

The first pair of reindeer slippers I ever bought was in Rovaniemi, in a tiny little shop called Lapin Nuket, which specialises in goods from Inari. Despite years of wear they are as good as ever, and in fact I'm wearing them as I write this. I can't say they are elegant: I now answer to 'Minnie Mouse', but I positively refuse to be parted from them.

It was in Rovaniemi too, along Koskikatu, that I found the joys of a hatter's shop in Finland. There, among the forestry caps, the small-brimmed pork-pie type of trilby beloved of Finnish men, and the furry ear-flapped winter hats equally dear to their hearts, I saw a pile of romantic, tall Cossack type

11 Winter in Helsinki: the Cathedral above the frozen harbour

reindeer fur hats, suitable for any winter princess. I tried them
all on and eventually settled for an elegant creamy creation. It
is wonderfully warm on a gusty January morning and ruins
every hairdo but I never wear it without thinking nostalgically
of my 'frontier town' for it is, after all, the little things that one
remembers most. The shop assistant who advised me to buy a
certain tablecloth, not as expensive as some of the others, all
made in the south of Finland, because, she said in her delightful
hissing English, 'thiss one, it never needss to have an iron,'
and she was right. And there was a pretty, fine-boned ladies'
hairdresser, hidden away at the back of the obviously male
preserve of a barber's shop, who didn't speak English or
Swedish but understood my pantomime immediately and
turned out a better job than many a London West End salon.
I've thought of her with some nostalgia in all sorts of corners
of the world since then! And then there was the little arty-
crafty loghouse on Pohjolankatu, where all the goods on sale
were made from pine or reindeer horn, and the calm-faced girl
in a handwoven skirt took time to show me all the most beautiful pieces, quite regardless of the fact that it was obvious that I
wasn't going to buy them. I was interested, so that was enough
. . . good manners and patience. On such foundations are the
tourist's goodwill balanced.

Perhaps the most outstanding building in Rovaniemi is the
Public Library. Designed by—guess who—Alvar Aalto, it is a
smooth, beautifully proportioned building, where one finds
books in every language and on every subject. Finns are in-
veterate readers and this library caters for every taste imagin-
able. Large quiet rooms and a lending library for art, where
one can borrow paintings or vases for limited periods, and a
lending library for music and recordings. But the most interesting thing was the room where serried ranks of chairs had ear-
phones and plugs, where people can sit and listen to lectures,
music, languages and children's stories. My eye fell on three
boys, no more than eight or nine years old, sitting unnaturally
quietly for that age group, enraptured by whatever was coming
through their headphones. Some time later that day I en-

countered the same three boys, transformed into Finnish 'Williams' creating their own brand of havoc near the sports ground, so they weren't really any different from boys elsewhere. But at least they were proving that they could concentrate and behave, on occasion. That library has stayed in my memory as one of the very best things in Finland. By the way, in the basement of the building there are two fascinating museums. One is devoted to birds indigenous or migratory to Finland, and the other has a fine collection of minerals. They are both rather special in their way. I preferred the minerals, for I have never liked to see birds anywhere but in the open air, flying, feeding and free, as the Almighty intended them to be. But I suppose that without such collections one couldn't protect or preserve the dwindling numbers that are still able to do all those things.

I came across the municipal camping site of Rovaniemi one day, beside the banks of the Ounasjoki, very close to the centre of the town. Behind it is the slope of Ounasvaara, where the Winter Games are held, and which now boasts a very pleasant motel. The site is well equipped, like most Finnish camping sites, and very popular in the summer months with visitors from all over the world. Lapland is, after all, a place for the open-air people, and campers and caravanners alike find their way to it, always stopping for a day or two to refuel and re-provision in 'The Gateway'. The river is clean, and ideal for swimming in the very hot weather that can be such a surprising feature of summer Lapland, although, alas, one can never depend upon it. Like many towns all over Scandinavia, Rovaniemi has its local history museum. This is at Poykkola, a farmhouse standing on its original site, which was bought by the Museum Society in 1957. There are fifteen buildings, housing all sorts of farm implements, mostly connected with salmon fishing and reindeer husbandry, both of which were once vital to the economy of the local farmers. It reminded me a bit of Maihaugen in Lillehammer in Norway. But at Poykkola there are a few items from prehistory, for as I have already said there have been people living in the north of Finland since the beginnings of time. If you should happen to be near Poykkola on the third Sunday in July in any year, go and try the fried salmon. They serve it to celebrate Marjetta Day. But if you are there at Midsummer, go and watch the log-riding on the Kemijoki instead. Then you'll really feel that the town is part of frontier country.

If you approach Rovaniemi by road from Kemi you will pass the area known as the Devil's Churns, some 21 kilometres before your destination. These are a series of potholes, supposedly the deepest in Finland. There is a flight of steps leading downwards, but don't try going down without permission. I had had enough of potholing in northern Norway, so I declined this one, but it is certainly worthy of note.

In a different context, you may like to visit the Norvajarvi Chapel, which is only a few kilometres from the centre of Rovaniemi. It stands over the graves of three thousand German soldiers who died in northern Finland.

The Polar Circle itself is marked by a little beflagged cottage where you can purchase souvenirs, stamps, etc., and have yourself photographed beside the reindeer in the enclosure. I don't know how many hundreds of people have stopped here. I heard a Frenchman ask one day if this was the North Pole, but I think it was just a case of faulty translation! After all, it is quite an achievement to have got this far north, and if you want to make an even bigger thing out of it, it is an idea to head slightly northeast, to Kemijarvi, and thence 43 lonely kilometres southwards to Suomutunturi, because the restaurant of the tourist hotel there lies right across the Polar Circle. It is an unusual place in any case, because the restaurant building is in the shape of a giant *kota*, or Lapp tent, with a great fireplace in the centre so that the smoke eddies from a central chimney.

The curtains are designed in the brilliant colours of the aurora borealis, and it is altogether a splendid place in which to enjoy some of the famous food of Lapland. *Tunturi* means 'hill', and when I went to Suomutunturi for the first time it was in the season of the *ruska*, the magnificent autumn of Lapland when the first frosts have pinched the cheeks of the earth until it seems to be afire, and yet still there is the afterglow of summer. My room looked out over the small lake at the foot of the hill which gives the place its name and which affords such splendid skiing terrain. The ski lift wasn't running, naturally, and one could almost hear the silence as the world seemed to be waiting for the advent of the first snows, which, from the leaden sky, couldn't be so far away; yet it was not cold, and I walked down from my verandah to the water's edge where it lapped gently against the stones. It was at that moment I think, that Lapland first began to cast its spell over me. To be able to find a sense of infinity within a few yards of a hotel balcony—how much more could I find if I looked?

Such was my ignorance of Lapland at this time that I thought this would be a very quiet place in the evening too. After all, it was literally miles from anywhere, so thought I, I'd go for a nice relaxing sauna before joining the hotel manager for a quiet dinner as I had been asked to do. But by the time I'd emerged rosy from the sauna, dressed and headed for the restaurant, I found that nearly every table was occupied, the candles were glowing, the log fire leaping skywards and that the band was playing beside the pint-sized dance floor (I'd learned enough about Finland to know that they'd be right up to date with the music anyway). Martti Kinnunen and his pretty wife, Anniki, smiled at my surprise. 'People travel long distances here in Lapland. We think nothing of 50 kilometres each way for an evening out. It doesn't take so long on our empty roads. Most of these people have come from Kemijarvi—apart from the resident guests like yourself of course. You will find as you travel that most of the Lapland hotels are very busy in the evenings, particularly at weekends, whether in winter or summer. But one member of the party must always stay completely sober to drive back. No alcohol for him, poor soul!'

By the time we'd polished off an excellent dinner, comprising sik, first cousin to the salmon, roast reindeer with cranberries and *suomuurain*, the golden, glowing, subtly flavoured cloudberries of the Arctic regions referred to earlier, covered with lashings of cream, the suggestion that I should go back with the Kinnunens to their home in Kemijarvi for coffee didn't seem so ridiculous. Only 43 kilometres . . . they brushed the distance (and the return journey to bring me back to the hotel) away as lightly as if it had meant going round to the corner shop. It was indeed a fast journey. We sped along the gravelled road at over 90 mph, and I wasn't at all surprised to learn that Martti's driving instructor had been one of the leading rally drivers in Finland. It only surprises me that more Finns aren't rally drivers (even if they secretly think they are in a Walter Mittyish sort of way!). They have the whole of the tundra to practise in. In no time we were at their cosy flat, meeting their daughters, Taina, Ritva, Sari and Outi, to say nothing of the poodle, Mira, drinking coffee and covering the world in our talk. The marvellous part about so many Finns is the fact that they really are interested in what happens in the world outside, and it seems that the further north they live, the more they know. Perhaps it is because of the long, dark days and nights when one must rely on books and the media, but I am inclined to think it is because they are intensely alive to the problems and difficulties of present-day living, and want to ensure that their children have a measure of safety, built on knowledge. Our evening had wings, but the highlight came on the way back to Suomutunturi, at about one a.m. We had been talking about the Northern Lights, or aurora borealis, that marvellous phenomenon of the northern skies, and I had asked if I could see them. 'Oh no,' they said, 'this is only fifteenth September. They don't come until after the heavy frost.' But there, faintly over the flat horizon came the pale ghostly green shadows, like long fingers in the night skies. Just one glimpse, and it was gone. The first indication that the *Kaamos*—the long twilight which envelops the northern hemisphere in winter—was not so very far away. My friends were amused at my excitement. 'Well,' they laughed, 'we do try always to please our guests in Finland.' I've seen many an aurora since, and I never cease to marvel at the eerie beauty of the dancers as they form their quadrilles in silver and green and red traceries which put the stars to flight, but it is always to my first glimpse of this wonder that my

thoughts return. Perhaps because of the people who, I am
partly convinced, ordered it all to happen for me.

Next morning, they presented me with a certificate which
says that I had crossed the Northern Polar Circle at 66° 33′
Northern Latitude, 28° 01′ Eastern Longitude. It also announces modestly at its foot that 'it was made from Lapponia
Pulp made by the Kemijarvi Pulp Mill'! This is part of the
fun of Lapland. It's like crossing the Equator—no matter how
many times you do it, it is still a novelty to be remembered and
enjoyed.

At this particular time in my love affair with Lapland, I had
yet to see my first reindeer. I had been warned that one of the
hazards of the long roads of Lapland are the reindeer herds
which stroll absent-mindedly across them, and whose protective
colouring is such that it is difficult to see them far ahead, so
when I set out from Suomu in my hired Renault to make my
way to another of the favourite holiday places of Lapland,
Pyhätunturi, at Pelkosenniemi, I was ready with camera and
brakes; but alas, again I was doomed to be disappointed, and
as it turned out on that trip it was to be in Swedish Lapland
and not in the Finnish area that I was eventually to catch up
with them. But Finland has relented to me very many times
since, and I'll come to that later.

Pyhätunturi lies some 45 kilometres northwest of Kemijarvi,
and is the southernmost of the mountain chains of northern
Finland, reaching to about 1,700 feet, not high by Scandinavian
standards. It is however, claimed to be among the oldest
mountains of the world because of the white sand found there,
said to have its origin in seas which must have covered the area
more than a thousand million years since. There is also a lot
of quartzite there, and in its markings are the traces of the
waves of those long vanished seas. Pyhätunturi has always been
a focal point for the religions, both heathen and Christian, and
indeed its name means 'holy mountain'. Since 1938 most of
the mountain chain has been part of a National Park Reserve,
and one of the most popular walks, for which one is advised
to have a guide unless very experienced in finding one's way

with compass etc., is to Pyhäkuru, an exceedingly beautiful canyon and to the holy waterfall above it, where the first local Lapps were christened.

Hotel Kultakero is situated just inside the treeline limit on the side of the fell, not very far from the tourist hotel and cabins. Its name, 'Golden Fell', comes from the small amount of gold once found in the area. Like many hotels in Finland its exterior presents an unexciting, even sombre face to the new arrival. Once through the door, however, one is immediately surrounded by the indefinable atmosphere of a Lapland hotel. Gay curtains, colourings and pictures, an open fire is never far away, and the smells of polish, coffee and warmth are a welcome in themselves, quite apart from the pleasantness of the reception staff. We trooped off down a long corridor, and arrived at my room. The corridors weren't as dark as at Suomu (dark passageways are very common in Scandinavian hotels which I feel is a deliberate policy to emphasise the contrast with the cheerfulness of the rooms). My room was certainly attractive: there was a steep drop on the hillside below my window, so there was no chance of stepping out there, unlike Suomu, but the view was magnificent across the tops of the green pines and firs to the other hills, still red with autumn, but with a pale sprinkling of white icing. From the huge dining-room windows one looked directly into the heart of the forest, rather like Lob's wood in *Dear Brutus*.

You can imagine my delight when, on my very first morning there, I was rewarded by the presence of a large mountain hare, his coat already showing patches of his winter white protective colouring, who sat calmly eating his own breakfast within a matter of inches from my table. We eyed each other speculatively for quite a time before, tiring of the process, he removed himself to pastures beyond my sight with a farewell flick of his tail, but it was rather wonderful to see a timid creature so unaffected by human presence. I went out into the woods, hoping to see him or his relations again, but no such luck. It was cold, and a bit wet underfoot, but so silent, and my noisy world was so far away. It would have been very easy to get lost out of sight of the hotel for all paths look alike to the inexperienced forest walker, but I stuck to the fringe of the forest, keeping the clear mountainside in sight on my left. I was asked later on what I would have done if I had seen a bear. 'Run' was all I could think of, then foolishly and naïvely, 'but I couldn't possibly have met one here, could I?' and my questioner laughed. 'Who knows in the forests of Lapland, but you are, regretfully right. There can only be between one and two hundred left in the whole of Lapland, and as for wolves . . . the Lapps have all but decimated them so that there are but a handful left.' I picked up a small piece of the white quartzite from the forest floor and took it back with me to the hotel. My new friends told me that the Saame use this to produce fire, striking one piece against the other until they produce a spark. It too, is just another of the precious souvenirs I have of this land that holds me in thrall.

The Finnish Tourist Office has been doing a formidable job on promoting Lapland for winter sports, and Pyhätunturi is well to the fore on this front with its illuminated slalom slopes, a chairlift, skilift and skischool. It is no wonder that Lapland is proving popular, because it does supply so many gentle slopes as well as ambitious ones, the hours of sun are long in spring and ski-touring, that wonderful form of skiing beloved of all Scandinavians, is so much easier to learn, even for un-athletic beings like myself. And there is always a pleasant, un-sophisticated, relaxed après-ski life. Hotel Kultakero was no exception to this, for, once again, coming from the sauna and the little swimming pool I found the hotel absolutely thronged with people intent on enjoying themselves, dancing to a band in full cry in a gay, natural atmosphere. It really is one of the many things about northern Finland that never ceases to astonish me—that in a land so bereft of humanity by day, there are always so many people at night!

But still no reindeer. After several wonderful days the snow started to arrive—at first, gently, delicately, but then thicker and fiercer until one couldn't see through its veil. I bewailed the lack of my longed-for quarry to my young hosts, and on my last evening, before retiring, said jokingly, 'Now, by the morning, before I leave, I do expect that you will have a reindeer standing beside the front door.' We all laughed and they promised to do their best. I had an early start, so my breakfast tray came to my room, bearing its usual substantial Finnish breakfast offerings of meat and cheese, rolls, pastry and fragrant coffee. But there was an addition. A small, toy, very lifelike reindeer stood among the food, with a label on his neck: 'We couldn't find a real reindeer in the time, but hope this will remind you of us.' He looks out now on the alien landscape of leafy Buckinghamshire, far from his native land, but for me, his very presence melts the mileage away . . .

The road runs northwards from Pyhätunturi to Luostotunturi and Sodankyla. It's worth stopping at the wooden church at the latter place because they discovered mummified remains there some years ago which proved the great age of the area. Surfaces were quite tricky for me in the newly fallen snows, for my car was still equipped with 'summer tyres' and not the pegged variety, but in the summer months this is a very pretty part of the country, with its hills and forests and the occasional river or lake. Luostotunturi is another of the modern ski resorts, and is distinguished by having Finland's longest skilift from the top of which there are magnificent views. I've dwelt so much on the autumn and winter look of Lapland, for these are my own favourites, that I have hardly mentioned what it looks like in summer, dressed in its Finnish uniform of dark green and blue. But this country is more brazen than its modestly clad neighbours in the south. Its grey hill shoulders are bare above the treeline to the midnight sun. Lapland midsummer is still exciting and stimulating to me. I find it difficult to sleep when the sun refuses to go to bed below the horizon, for I hate heavy curtains at windows, and my body still works on the principle that if the sun's up, I must be up too. Mind you, it is overdoing it a bit when one hears, as I have done, lawnmowers being used in a small garden at three in the morning, in the lands of the midnight sun! Northern peoples on the whole do live up to the principle 'we have all winter to sleep', but when I remember the winter gaiety already mentioned, I begin to wonder if that is strictly true either. I remember asking a stout middle-aged lady who presided over the small restaurant at the top of a skilift elsewhere in Lapland what she would be doing in the coming winter, and she replied, with a twinkle in her eyes: 'Why, go the village and make love of course! What else is there to do!' and I didn't think she was entirely kidding . . . ! In recent times, the Finns, enterprising and practical people that they are, have been making a big thing out of the fact that the winter in Lapland is perfect for honeymooners. Long nights—what couple could resist four months when they may as well stay in bed? But the *Kaamos* is not dark, it is the most romantic and beautiful time, and that may be equally important. You see, even though the sun doesn't actually appear *above* the horizon for six to eight weeks, there is a reflection of light, like a constant twilight. Add the brilliance of the white snow to this, plus the moonlit nights, the clarity of the stars (for one sees so very many on the clear frosty nights of the north) and above all, the awesome, unearthly aurora borealis, and one has a considerable amount of light. Very much more in fact, than one gets on a grey winter day in the industrial towns of central England, when the fog is low and the sky is dark with threatened rainclouds. Nevertheless, the constant diet of 'darkness' and lack of sun does cause a rather special form of sickness—Arctic sickness—people get depressed easily, particularly by the end of the *Kaamos*, and it does definitely have an effect on the natures of the peoples who live out their lives in these latitudes. Nowadays, vitamins can help enormously to replace the deficiencies, but so too, do the package holidays to the Canary Islands which are run so cheaply from all the northern countries! You can't tell me that the growth of tourism of this kind hasn't brought tremendous benefits in the most unexpected areas.

Summer in Lapland is often surprisingly warm, though this can't be relied upon. I've been as long as a month in the north when the temperature hasn't fallen below 70 degrees, but once it breaks one can never be sure when it will be fine again. Maybe

tomorrow and maybe in two months' time! One odd thing
about northern summers is the fact that even though I find it
difficult to sleep, whether hotelling, camping or caravanning,
the day birds, sensible creatures, certainly don't. They stop
singing at the normal sunset hours—well a bit later, say around
nine or ten p.m.—and don't start again until very early
morning. The night birds work shorter shifts, but I could wish
that more of them would stay awake and develop a liking for
feeding on the mosquito which is such a pest of the north in
summer months. I'm lucky because mosquitoes really don't like
me very much, but for sufferers they can be hell, and the only
efficacious remedy that I have ever found for my family is to
burn mosquito coils at the door of the tent or on the verandah
of the bedroom. Even on the running waters of the great rivers
they are a nuisance, both to the would-be fisherman, or to the
increasing number of would-be goldpanners who make their
way up to Tankavaara each year.

This is terrific fun. You aren't likely to make a fortune, but
the very possibility of making even a few grains of gold appear
in the dirt of your sifting pan gets into your blood like fever. It
has become quite a tourist attraction these days, but for some
people, not tourists at all, it is a way of life each summer. There
is one man, away up on the Lemmenjoki, who spends each of
his summers panning for gold. He goes mainly for the pleasure
of the silence, the freedom, and the sheer beauty of calling his
soul his own. He has rigged his own special systems of sifting,
as well as using the old panning methods, and he is reluctant to
say what he makes. 'Not a fortune,' he says, 'but enough to
allow me to afford to come each year.' And in the winter? He
shrugged. 'I go back to being a tramdriver in Helsinki.' He
perhaps, has found the real recipe for living. One doesn't need
all the trappings of civilisation, not all the time at least, and I
noticed that the mosquitoes too, lived in comparative amity
with him.

But I suppose the mosquito are really the province of the
fish, and are part of the reason why Lapland is such a paradise
for the sport fishermen, who are to be seen everywhere, sitting

patiently like statues, in little boats in centres of lakes, or wading in rivers, oblivious to everything but the pursuit of their prey. Certainly the passion is infectious. It was very early one summer morning that I hooked my first trout, after the most inexpert cast you ever saw. I could hardly reel it in for excitement and nearly fell off the slippery wet rock. Then, when it finally arrived, I unhooked it, very carefully, and put it back in the river. Well, I felt sorry for the poor little thing. It was small, and maybe it would learn its lesson, and anyway, it took my appetite away when I thought of its freedom before I came. Maybe it would have been different if I had been hungry. Incidentally there are two artificial lakes about a hundred kilometres north of Sodankyla. These have become quite a feature of Finnish fishing, and these two are kept very well stocked so one stands a chance of getting good fish.

Anyone intending to take fishing gear with them to Finland can have a wonderful time, but do check with local authorities on where to go, what permit is required and what restrictions may be in force, such as whether one can fish with the motor running, or the use of spoons, or imitation fish bait and so forth, for the fish are, quite rightly, protected by the Finns and there are a number of regulations governing sport fishing both by Finns and foreigners. Everyone needs a permit. It is valid for one year and each family may have only one permit, though all the names of the members of each family who are intending to fish may be entered on it. But if you are under sixteen you can fish without a permit. I guess the powers that be don't consider that a youngster is likely to have the experience to take a big catch. Also, as far as I can see, though I may be wrong, you don't need a permit to fish if using worms as bait. Maybe Finnish fish don't like worms! Anyway, check up, just to be on the safe side. A mistake is not likely to cause an international incident, but it wastes precious holiday time, and there are also special regulations governing camping and fishing, automobile tourist licences for fishing, and ice-fishing. Nowadays there are a number of package holidays which are arranged by travel companies within Finland which include fishing trips, so that many of the whys and wherefores are painlessly extracted. Finnair, for instance, take would-be ice-fishermen to Lake Inari in March, April and May, where they can stay in a wilderness cabin or in a tourist hotel. Ice-fishing is the exciting pastime, known in Finnish as *pilkkionginta*, in which one fishes through a hole bored in the ice.

Pilkkionginta. Isn't it a lovely word? Like so much of the Finnish language, purely descriptive. To date, ice-fishing has been a pastime strictly for the Scandinavians, or others born in a similar climate, but each year a few foreigners get hooked along with the fish, and interest is growing, though it is a cold old business, even in the warmth of the spring sun, when one can get a magnificent tan from the reflection of the sun on the ice. The surface of the lakes freezes to a considerable depth in winter, sometimes more than eighteen inches, and it doesn't let the light through, so that during this time the fish are deprived of light and of oxygen. When a fisherman bores a hole in the ice, it lets the oxygen in and the fish quite naturally come to it. Not fair on the fish? No, but fun for the fisherman! There are even big annual competitions now, organised by the central organisation of Finnish fishermen. There's a starting signal and then they all rush off to the ice to choose their spots, bore holes with a special tool for the purpose, and start fishing. After a specified time the catch is weighed in. There are some pretty substantial prizes to match the catches. But, equally, one sees an ice-fisherman, lonely in the middle of his frozen lake, completely content in his isolation, absorbed in what he is doing to the exclusion of all else. I'm always amused to notice the pads of newspaper, or perhaps straw, on which they stand to protect their feet. A Lapp now, he usually uses reindeer skin. Reindeer again . . .

North of Sodankyla one is coming to the district of Inari, among the most famous of all Lapp strongholds. Surely, the Lapps are among the world's most exotic people. Short, dark, Slavic in bone structure, the older people often bow-legged due to the lack of vitamins in their diet as children, while even many of the present-day youngsters have poor teeth; understood by few, even in Scandinavia, forgotten by most of the world, they are nevertheless extremely important if one wants to know something of how man can triumph over the hardships of living in sub-zero temperatures for much of every year. The Lapp or, to give him his preferred name, Samek ('Saamelaisek' in Finnish), has his own language or languages, for there are a number of dialects, such as northern or mountain Lappish, Inari Lappish and Skolt Lappish in Finland, and several others in Norway and Sweden as well. Finnish and Lappish have some similarities, but they cannot be said to be so alike as to make understanding possible. The lack of knowledge of the Lapp languages has led to many difficulties all over Scandinavian Lapland for Lapp children because, until recently, there was a shortage of books in Lappish and an even bigger shortage of Lappish-speaking teachers. It is improving, so that one hopes the languages will be retained, at least in the younger age groups. In later education the Lapp children have to learn in the tongue of the particular country in which they live and very few take their school-leaving examinations in their mother Lappish. These peoples of the north, have, as might be expected, many words which apply to nature around them, for they are so completely bound up with the climate in which they must live.

They are surely among the oldest peoples in Europe, probably dating back eight thousand years, and may well have been confused with the 'Fenni' discovered by Tacitus, but their ways can have changed very little over the ages until comparatively recently. In the Middle Ages it is known that Finns bartered with the Lapps, and it was in Gustavas Wasa's time in the sixteenth century that the Lapps were ordered to pay their taxes direct to the crown and that it was decreed that the wilderness lands belonged to 'God, to us and to the Swedish Crown'. It was during the seventeenth century that the Lapps turned away from being mainly hunters and fishers to herders of reindeer and began the nomadism that has remained ever since. It may be linked to Gustavas Wasa's decree, but it is more likely that it was because the wild reindeer was on the decrease and the Lapp began his own conservation programme in sheer necessity of survival; it may too have been connected with the fact that the Finns were colonising the North. Lapps are still notorious for not liking to be too near other people. Anniki Setala relates a story to the effect that when a Saame saw some wood shavings floating down a stream he snapped out, 'No peace any more if they are going to build so close to me.' The house was nearly 100 miles away!

By the mid-eighteenth century the age-old rights of the Lapps were being whittled away, and nowadays the Lapp Right still exists in Sweden and Norway, but in a limited form. This Lapp Right bestows upon its holders privileges regarding land use, fishing and hunting in connection with his main occupation, but if a Lapp moves away from his village in Sweden to buy land as a farmer he loses the Lapp Right and cannot regain it. Very much more is being done to protect the interests and opinions of the Lapp communities within Finland, and young Lapps, better educated than their elders, are also taking a much greater interest in the political and economic future. There are associations within each of the Laplands to protect Lapp interests and these are very much alive and extremely vociferous on occasion, and also there is the Nordic Council, which covers the entire area and has met regularly for twenty years. There has been a suggestion that the question of the Lapp language should be placed before the United Nations, though at the time of writing I cannot discover just how far that has got.

Lapland is rather an economic backwater when it comes to comparison with the rest of Finland, partly due to climate, partly due to terrain, but mostly due to the fact that even in the best of times there is very little employment apart from the small farms, and inevitably this has meant a steady drift southwards. When I asked what could be done about this during a private conversation I was answered by: 'Well, if there are less people up here, it will mean less lives to be lost if the Russians come back again . . .', but I feel that that was a purely personal view which stemmed from bitter experience, and is not the general opinion.

12   The 'survival kit' of the Lapps

13 (above) Gold panning on the Lemmenjoki River

14 A journey behind the poro *entails wearing a heavy reindeer-skin coat.*

There has been talk of a huge hydro-electric scheme involving the River Kemi, but if this does come eventually into complete operation it will mean flooding a considerable area of swampy land where the reindeer graze. This has actually happened in some places elsewhere and in consequence there has been bitterness and antagonism from the dwindling number of reindeer-herding Lapps. One can well appreciate their natural anxieties, for already, with the restricted areas for winter grazing, herds have been having a bad time for the past few winters and losses have been quite heavy. One could point to tourism as the New Messiah which would automatically bring new roads and improved conditions and could help to preserve the old ways if it becomes the main occupation, but this too has its opponents, and although a few make their living from tourism in the form of souvenirs, guiding, etc., many Lapps actively resent having their photographs taken, and not un-naturally dislike being looked upon as curiosities. They are afraid too, of the damage that a thoughtless few could do. For instance, a noisy skidoo or snomobile used by a tourist intent on his photographs could frighten reindeer cows in calf, so that they drop their young before time, and again there would be loss of income because, of course, the Lapp relies very much on the number for slaughter each year. I was told by a forester near Enontekio that the use of skidoos, snowcats, etc., is restricted to farmers, Lapps and foresters and they are not available to tourists, but this may not always be possible to control if tourism increases, purely because of the vastness of the terrain. One would hate to think that these nasty noisy machines which have become so much of a way of life for pleasure purposes in countries like northern Canada, could be, however un-consciously, the means of bringing the final coup de grâce to the silences of the Lapp provinces.

The nomadic life is being followed less and less in any case, as the years progress. Most Lapps in Finland live in small communities in modern housing now, so that the children may be educated; they can have television (a doubtful advantage perhaps), receive their newspapers (of which there is incidentally one in Lappish, *Sabmelas*, printed eight times a year and distributed free to all Lapp families in Finland) and listen to their own Lapp programmes on the radio. The men travel to and from the grazing grounds by snomobiles instead of travelling with their herds by reindeer-drawn *pullka*, taking the entire family and living in the *kota*, the tepee-type of tent made from wooden birchpoles and covered with thick woollen blankets, though in summer the young men usually live on the edge of the pastures to care for the herds from there. The community life is certainly helping with the children's chances in later life. Some become doctors, teachers and nurses, others follow the natural artistic bents and develop as artists and specialists in the folklore and arts of their people, such as the unaccompanied voice chants of the Lapp, known as *joik* or *juigo*. None of this, or very little, would have been possible while the tribes were constantly on the move.

There is one community however, who keep very much to their own ways and traditions and hardly integrate even with other Lapps. The Skolt Lapps used to live in the Petsamo region, but during the war, they were moved over to Ostrobothnia for safety. However, when the Continuation War ended with the u.s.s.r.'s victory, their former lands were part of the reparation price which had to be paid to Russia, so the Skolts were resettled at Sevettijarvi, reached on a poor road from Inari. They are still there, speaking their own dialect and worshipping in their own way, for they are mostly members of the Orthodox Church, unlike most Lapps. There are only about six hundred of them in the settlement, and I understand that they still receive special help from the Finnish Government, because they remain among the underprivileged whose living conditions are not as good as could be wished for. Their own customs, language and even clothing distinguish them from other Lapps, but it could be that the much despised tourism could, in the end, be their salvation, *if* used in the right and understanding ways to which it has been put elsewhere in Finland. The education towards this has of course, to be directed towards the Skolt himself, so that he will not look upon himself as a curiosity, but as a defender of the last bastions of the old, much respected and much prized ways. Not easy to accomplish, but the Finns have overcome bigger problems than this in their history, so they will tackle this too. But time is not on their side.

Most Lapps belong to the rather austere, severe cult of Laestadism, started by a Christian missionary, Lars Levi Laestadius in the 1840s. It has very strict standards of morality, condemning everything which is not in accordance with biblical teachings. It allows confession, and in fact this plays a very great part in the practice of the religion. Before the advent of Christianity the Lapps practised a shamanistic religion, based in the natural phenomena of sun, earth, fire and the elements and which relied greatly on the ecstatic fervours it created with its drums. The shaman or witch doctor passed into a trance and then was supposed to be able to communicate with the world of the dead to find out the best places for hunting or to see the future. Like all the old religions there were places where women were forbidden to tread; is the present restriction on women clergy in some sections of the Christian churches a throwback to these beliefs?

The early missionaries succeeded in stamping out the shamanism in a remarkably short time. I asked one day what happened when, for instance, some old diehards had wanted to stay in their own heathen religions because they were too old to change. 'Killed off,' came the nonchalant reply. So much for Christian charity and freedom to worship how and where one would, in those not so far-off days.

Now one can see many items from the old religions, some real, some reconstructed. Most of the old everyday utensils have vanished, some of them into museums like the fascinating one at Inari, but some Lapp families have special things of their own, handed down through the years and although not used, prized and kept. In one immaculate little wooden homestead, complete with every modern convenience of dishwasher, laundry, deep-freeze, etc., I was shown a small wooden cradle, still with its brightly coloured decorations, designed to keep away evil spirits from the child. It was at least a hundred years old, but every baby in the family had spent some time in it. The same man showed me beautifully worked reindeer horn knives, which had belonged to his father and grandfather, and some needles and bobbins, made from reindeer bone, which had been used by the women of the family who worked as they walked in the long migrations behind the reindeer.

And so one always comes back to the reindeer, which has for so long provided the Saame with food, clothing, working implements, decorations and money. When I first saw a reindeer, running along beside the train on the way from Kiruna in Sweden to Narvik in Norway, I was impressed, as I have been on many occasions since, by the grace of the animals, for in spite of their unwieldy-looking spade-shaped hooves, designed to scrape away at the snow to uncover the green-grey lichen which forms their staple diet, they have a long steady lope and cover the bare ground at quite a rate. But it isn't until one sees them moving over the snow that one realises just how cleverly Nature has designed them, enabling them to keep their balance and keep going even through snowdrifts and over 'rotten' snow, that is, the snow which is beginning to melt with the advent of spring, but which still appears to be sound. And they still have the edge over the skidoos, because the animal itself has the knack of finding its way, which a machine cannot do. A friend of mine opted for a sno-scooter when working in Lapland several winters ago, drove it towards snow which he had thought was quite solid, and then took several hours to dig himself and the vehicle out! It was with some chagrin that while so occupied, he watched heavily laden sledges, drawn by reindeer, negotiating almost identical territory, floundering, struggling, but nevertheless getting through. He said afterwards that his admiration for the beast increased with every spadeful of snow he dug!

It was from Enontekio, some 80 miles from the Norwegian border, that I first experienced the tremendous thrill of driving behind the reindeer on my own sledge. There is a reindeer-driving school at Rovaniemi, the only one of its kind in the

world, but I hadn't attended that, and instead elected to go
out, untried, with a Lapp guide on what has now become
known as a 'reindeer safari'. Since that time these have become
quite a feature of Lapland tourist life and their popularity is
growing fast. They can only be taken in a limited period of the
year, that is Arctic spring, when the sun is warmer but the snow
is still deep. I make no apologies for the fact that I am very
proud that I was the first British woman journalist to make the
journey and I long to do it again, just as soon as I can, but for
much, much longer.

'*Poro*' is both Finnish and Lapp for reindeer. My *poro* safari
was to begin from Jussenstupa, a small tourist hotel in Enontekio, some 300 kilometres inside the Arctic Circle. There is
another hotel there, at Hetta, right beside the lake—but when
it is frozen one cannot tell where the land begins and the water
starts—Jussenstupa is very simple, but cosy, and with superb
breakfasts including the magnificent porridge which is so often
served in the north, meat, eggs, fish and of course coffee and
buttermilk. The sun had woken me at about 5 a.m. when the
only sign of life seemed to be the magpies chattering noisily
against a clear blue sky, but by the time I'd made the most of
my breakfast and was ready for collection—between eight and
nine they'd told me, but one can never be sure of time with
Lapps, for they might come, or they might not—a white frosted
mist had descended and one could see nothing at all. Then he
loomed out of the shadow, an exotic figure in his blue and red,
with ropes slung cowboy fashion over his shoulder and formidable knives at his waist. He led the way to the *pulkas*, where the
reindeer stood ready in the traces, their breath adding to the
mist around us. He rummaged in a pile of furs on one of the
pulka and indicated that I should put a huge garment made of
skins over my own clothes. This proved no easy matter for I
was already wearing, apart from warm underwear, two
sweaters, a sheepskin jacket, ski-pants and heavy boots. Nevertheless, I did as I was bid and felt like an overstuffed armchair.
He also found me a pair of reindeer-skin boots, so I took off
my own and replaced them with the skin ones. I scrambled on

to my sledge, covering myself with even more reindeer skins, tucked my gloved hands inside the furs, together with my cameras, and we were off into the gloom.

We had one reindeer per sledge, each fastened by wooden traces with stout leading reins made of ox and reindeer skin. My *poro* had only one antler, which gave him rather a rakish look, while the others varied between a full set and none at all. Their colouring too, varied from dark grey to creamy white. Esa Kaupilainen, the Lapp, knelt on one knee upon the first sledge, and we moved in line behind him using his tracks almost exactly. It was completely silent, unearthly almost, apart from the scrunching of wood against the ice and the regular squeaking rhythm of the reindeer hooves across the snow. It's a strange noise—once you've heard it it can never be mistaken again for anything else. We plodded up hills and hurtled down the far sides, with the *poro* floundering Disneywise in the soft snow but miraculously keeping us upright in spite of the crazy swaying of our sledges; we scraped over the ice of the frozen lakes and rivers, plunged into frosted forests where the ice hung like flowers around us and the only sound was the deep-throated growl of Esa as he guided his beasts, while the sun struggled like a lost lamp in the eerie grey of the swirling mists, until, without warning, it burst through in a sapphire sky, and the winter wonderland of the north in all its lonely majesty was mine for the taking. It wasn't all white . . . it was every hue of blue and violet and yellow where the sun struck the ice in a brilliance which hurt the eyes and forced one to wear the sun-glasses hidden in the bottom of the camera cases. My hands were, by this time, completely numb, for I had had gloves off and on to photograph and my fingers had become useless in seconds—I soon learned that one *can* fiddle with cameras with gloves on!

We stopped at one hut on the way for a few moments, mainly to let me see the cabin, which was just one of the many one finds in these wilderness lands for the comfort and welfare of travellers both in winter and summer. They are only small, roughly furnished with plain wooden furniture, but always with chopped wood, ready for a fire to be made, and often with a small stock of food. The only proviso about using such cabins is that one must leave the place in perfect order and with sufficient wood chopped for the next traveller. Some huts even have telephones. I haven't used one of them, but I do know that two journalist friends of mine, a Belgian and a Frenchman, had taken the opportunity to telephone their homes in Brussels and Paris during a summer visit the year before! So the wilderness is not always quite so isolated as one would perhaps like to believe.

We stopped to rest the animals in the now very warm sunshine by another hut and talked to some skiers we found taking advantage of the hut, its facilities and a breathing space before continuing their cross-country tour. My Lapp friends used another hut, close by, to prepare our lunch. *Poronkaristys*—reindeer stew—very rich and made from reindeer and pork and ice-water. We cheated, because we had brought packets of dried potatoes with us; there was no such luxury in the old days. The stew was very satisfying and extremely tasty, and we washed it down with light Finnish beer and a nip from a flask of Drambuie hidden also among my reindeer skins. But my guide, Esa, refused that. 'I'll wait until I get home,' he said . . . drunk in charge of a reindeer? Perhaps, but far more likely is the fact that most Lapps will not allow themselves to take alcohol when working because many have a reputation for fighting when a drink is inside them. It has been the curse of Lapland. Esa, sensible fellow, was taking no chances on anything. I took the opportunity of the stop to ask Esa (through another companion who spoke some English, for Esa had no other language than Lappish) about his reindeer. I was of course careful not to ask how many he had, because that would have been tantamount to asking him outright how much money he had in the bank (somewhat in the same way that one never asks a Cretan on the plain of Lassithi how many windmills he has). He was most patient with my questions, and told me that he had to sell about forty animals a year to live, and that at that time an animal on the hoof would fetch about £70. He also said that because Finnish Lapps were not allowed to move their animals about in the same way as the Norwegian Lapps, there was much difficulty in grazing. In the areas he used the reindeer moss was very short, whereas on the Norwegian frontiers it grew much taller. There had been too much overgrazing and it had led to starvation among the reindeer and consequent loss. He was carrying sacks of the grey-green lichen for his animals on this trek, and fed them at each stop. However, he said, if the summer was good they would soon put on the lost condition. I had tried to put my hand out towards one of them, to stroke it, but it had shied away, still half wild, and had upset the sledge, so I didn't try that again, and yet I saw one of the animals, a beautiful gentle-eyed creamy creature, nuzzling to one of the Lapp women who accompanied us. It was apparently a particularly affectionate creature and unusual. 'He even likes bread,' they laughed. 'But we don't encourage that, except in the leading beasts, who are always brought up in the more domesticated atmosphere so that we can command them, and then the others will follow them.' I asked if it was ever necessary to call a vet for the animals. Esa shook his head, smiled and pointed to his knife. It was answer enough.

The overnight stop was in one of the aforementioned shelter huts, where *poro* skins did duty for eiderdowns and the room smelt sweetly of birch and pinewood, and breakfast was of the thick rye porridge with melted butter and sugar, and smoked *poro* and coffee. Reindeer is very filling and tasty in all its forms, but as a permanent diet it would get a bit tiresome I think. That is when the *pilkkionginta* comes into its own! And nowadays there are modern deep-freeze cabinets in the villages . . .

Evening was wonderful. Dark violet shadows lengthened across the bumpy surfaces of the frozen lakes until gradually the sky was first saxe blue, then almost black and the great stars hung low above us. There was no moon that night, and it clouded over, but it was exquisitely beautiful and unbelievably peaceful outside the cabin, while, inside, the cheerful fire burned and there was laughter and *joik*, at which we all tried our hands.

Next day, while on trek, we stopped by a *kota*, which had been erected specially for us by one of the foresters and another Lapp, so that it too, was cheating really, but it was exactly of the type which are used everywhere in the north, including the nature trails across Sweden and Finland taken by hundreds of walkers each year, so I didn't feel too badly about it. The men made a fire inside it, on the snow, just as I had seen one made many times before in northern Norway to smoke the reindeer meat, and we grilled reindeer steaks in its embers and made coffee, sitting on the snow as near as possible to the blaze and kippering ourselves in the process. Reindeer is lean, so it was good, eaten from the sticks, along with *makkara* (sausages), another inseparable item of food from the daily diet in Finland, though not strictly Lappish! Again the sun had shown his face to us, the sky was deep blue and the snow had taken on a pale golden tint which was breathtaking in its delicacy. Our reindeer lay comfortably still in their traces, nibbling at the snow for moisture, and eating the moss that again, Esa had placed beside each animal. I would have liked to have another try at petting my obliging animal, but didn't dare to repeat the chaos of yesterday, for it had meant broken traces and a repair job. Esa told me that it takes years to train an animal to pull a sledge and seldom were they very willing about it. One can't blame them. They are used for everything. Food, clothing, trading, transport—not one iota of any beast is ever wasted, right down to the gut, used for sewing the skins, and the tongues, a special and very expensive delicacy in the south of Finland.

I got back to Jussenstupa with regret. I had to go back to my own civilisation, though I much preferred Esa and Johann's, at least for a while. The little scheme which these men run does show their visitors just a little of what it is like to live in the north, even though there are other forms of transport now. These forward-looking Lapps don't want hordes of visitors; they couldn't cope with them if they had them, but they want to maintain their links with the old ways, while shaking hands with the new. Reindeer have always been the salvation of the Saame peoples. Perhaps in this small corner of Finnish Lapland they have yet another use, by helping their masters to accept more of the inevitable encroachment of the modern world, while showing us, the outsiders, just a small glimpse of the silent, beautiful, forgotten country which is one of the last wildernesses in Europe.

But I hadn't yet left Enontekio, and it had one more surprise for me. After dinner that evening, which is always early in Lapland, I was asked if I'd like to go to a dance. 'Why not?' said I. 'Well, we'll walk,' they said, 'It isn't too far, and then we can drink too.' So, on went the boots, the ski-pants, the top coats, but not mercifully, my coat of reindeer skins and we set off in the starry, icy night. We walked, or rather picked our way carefully on the slippery roads for about an hour, and quite honestly I couldn't see a sign of life anywhere and was beginnng to wonder if this was all some snare and delusion. Then we turned off down a narrow path towards a small house on a hill, which looked quite deserted. Up some steps to a side door, opened it and hey presto! a full-size discothéque which would have done justice to the West End of London! Only instead of dolly-bird dresses and smooth jackets, these people were wearing an assortment of clothes which varied from skirts and blouses, sweaters and ski-pants and delight of delight, full Lapp dress. Seeing a Lapp in a disco did my heart a power of good! It really was a swinging place, dancing, drinking, gaiety, completely modern, good drinks—expensive but good measures—excellent open sandwiches—perhaps this was the most surprising place I found in all my wanderings in Finnish Lapland. I lost my heart to Enontekio, to its impressive church, to its courteous, yet so helpful people, to Esa, Johann and the family who were so kind, and to one special creamy reindeer. I don't think I could bear to think that I had seen it all for the last time. In my mind I go back there as often as I can, to try and recapture just a little of the peace and tranquillity.

For the visitor—indeed, for the Lapps themselves—the winter roundups are the most important dates on the calendar, for they provide the meeting place for families who might not meet again until the following year. It is during these roundups that one sees the need for the lariat for, as I have said, the reindeer can move quite fast, and one also sees the need for the dogs, who perform almost the same tasks as the sheepdogs in the Welsh and Scottish hills. The snow swirls as it is churned upwards by thousands of the spade-shaped hooves and the tug of war begins when a lariat descends over an animal's neck and it is dragged towards its owner's corral to be checked or branded, or perhaps slaughtered. How each man knows his own animals among so many is still a mystery to those of us to whom all reindeer look alike! But there are differences and slowly I am beginning to see them. When an animal is to be slaughtered on the spot it is an astonishingly quick merciful process, instantaneous because the knife is used in the neck at the back of the head. Better perhaps than the humane killer of the slaughterhouse, for there is no long travelling to the place of death, sensed by so many animals. The fear in the eyes is not there for nearly so long. Carcasses are cleaned and hung in the freezing air, which forms its own refrigerator, to await the buyers. Other animals are chosen to be used for work around the settlements and are castrated to make them easier to handle. Calves are sorted, branded and finally turned loose with the rest to wander free for another year. There is little noise. Even the Spitz dogs work silently and the whole spectacle is immensely impressive.

It isn't always easy to photograph these happenings, for although they are a joy to the beholder they can be a headache to the photographer. Too much light, or too little. It takes even more time and patience than elsewhere, but the results are worth waiting for. Lapps, as I have already said, are not too keen on being photographed, but they suffer the tourist reasonably well at the roundups and I've always found them to be very co-operative. Private occasions are, however, rather different. One just shouldn't barge in and photograph all and sundry without a little polite enquiry first. Saame costume is worn on high days and holidays and also on many workdays, but the full glory of the headdresses cannot be seen unless there is a special occasion, for then the mass of ribbons at the back is allowed to fly freely, and the headdress of the Four Winds is a most beautiful thing, transforming the highly practical clothing into magnificence, especially when accompanied by the beautiful jewellery worn by many Saame women as part of their dowry. Again, one doesn't ask too much about this. It just isn't polite. After all, it isn't only in Lapland that a people puts wealth into its animals and into the jewellery of its women-folk. But in winter, all too often, again as a matter of practicality you will see many wearing the fur coats and boots which helped to make my own trip so memorable, and it is brought back yet again that it is the reindeer who is the real hero of Lapland, with his supporting cast of the 2,500 or so Saame who have their origins in this land of nowhere.

There is, at the time of writing, an entirely new scheme being sponsored by Matkatoimisto Erämatkat, in Rovaniemi, for taking parties of upwards of ten people to see the autumn round-ups, one in September, two in October and one in November. This is aimed mainly at the Finnish market for, of course, many Finnish people have never even set foot in the land of the Saame but at the same time, the promoters hope that foreigners will come. They are proposing to make them of a four-day duration, and because reindeer, wind, weather (and Lapps!) are not entirely predictable, have laid on a series of other occupations of purely Lapland character to occupy the 'waiting' time for the big event. One can only admire the initiative behind the idea and wish them every success, at least in trying to bring some extra money to the area. I cannot envisage that the roundups could ever become a sort of Calgary of the north. Heaven forbid; but the nature of the people involved would see to that. There has even been talk of letting people join in, but again, unless one was a sort of John Wayne with a lasso, or had some skill in holding on to the horns of a recalcitrant reindeer while it was being branded, I think the main fascination would be for the camera enthusiast, or for the person intent on capturing the very special flavour of a new experience. The main danger would be, whether you went on a scheme like this one in the cocoon of a safe party or on your own, that you would catch Lapland Fever, so that, like me, you would be drawn inevitably back again and again to this strange, empty, lonely, fearsome, and yet so completely full and beautiful land.

I'll end this chapter in the only way I can, by taking you along the romantically named 'Way of the Four Winds', from Muonio. Muonio has a modest but comfortable little hotel at Olostunturi, run by a mountain of a man called Arvo Yliniemi, whose pride and joy is his swimming pool, opened in 1971. There is a camping site near the hotel, and somehow Mr Yliniemi finds time to talk to people up there too—but then people always have time for their visitors in Lapland. Then on by Haltiatunturi, Finland's highest mountain (4,000 feet) along the side of Kilpisjarvi Lake, to the place where the Norwegian, Swedish and Finnish Laplands meet. There isn't much to be seen there. No barbed wire and fierce guards. No drama. Just a simple granite stone, a long, weary but beautiful journey from the capitals of the three countries it represents. Yet, it is indicative of the way in which these three northern neighbours live: quietly, in amity, in understanding, in friendship, in hope of lasting peace. One of my greatest treasures is a small garnet which was picked up among the tumbled stones near the Lemmenjoki. It is still in its unpolished state, just as nature made it, but I have set it in gold. It has little commercial value, but it has a deep red glowing heart hidden within its rough exterior, and to me it represents the ferocity, the beauty, the torment and the peace, the gentleness and the honesty of Lapland.

5. Westwards

There was a fresh wind blowing from the sea as I drove down the long peninsula towards Hanko, the southernmost town in Finland, and the skies were that special steely blue that one so often gets across these waters at the mouth of the Gulf. A fitful sun hid its face under a grey handkerchief, and by the time I pulled up beside the eastern harbour where a dozen or so small boats rocked at their moorings, there was more than a hint of rain in the air. But there was a sweet clean tang too, and the song of the yacht stays was not a mournful one—rather it told of great days at sea and the excitement of being under sail. It told too of the days when the last of Britain's 'wooden walls' passed by these shores during the fierce engagements of the Crimean War, too often forgotten by the historians who prefer to dwell on the soldiers' battles in the south and the justifiably lauded achievements of Miss Nightingale and her band. I had stopped in Tammisaari on the way down, better known during that terrible war as Ekenas, and had been shown the cannonball fired by the English fleet (one of a number of such relics on these coasts), but it was Hanko which I desired to visit most, to try and recapture some of the atmosphere of yesterday, and the day before.

And it wasn't all that difficult. In spite of the fact that Hanko, or Hango, to give it both its Finnish and Swedish names, was almost completely destroyed in the Second World War, and has been rebuilt like so many other towns in Finland in highly modern style, there are traces of the old town and seaside resort so much beloved by wealthy Russians under Tsarist rule. On the road which runs behind the tennis courts overlooking the bathing beach there are more than a few houses which betray the Russian influence. One can imagine the leisured, relaxed atmosphere of the town in those days, so far removed from the frenetic, gossip-ridden, suspicion-filled life which surrounded the Russian Imperial court. No wonder everyone from the Tsars downward liked to make their way into the Grand Duchy of Finland during the magic summers of the white nights. No wonder too when one looks at the map, that Hango was considered by the Russians to be vital to their defences during the Second World War, for it stretches out its neck to see everything that is going on in the Baltic and in the Gulf itself. And it has always been that way, providing an anchorage and a calling point for centuries for seamen on their way between east and west, whether on law-abiding or more nefarious missions.

In those days it was the small Kapelhamnen on the northern side of the peninsula which was in everyday use, and up to the seventeenth century there was a chapel there, which of course gave the place its name. That has gone, but nearby there is still a strange rock formation from the Ice Age, called in today's parlance a 'kettle'. It, at least, survived the wars, the fires and man's destruction. During the Middle Ages another harbour was used on the island of Tullhomarna, and on the sides of the narrow channel between two islands of rock called Godtarmen it was the custom for the merchants, soldiers and sailors to carve their names and their coats of arms as they waited for a fair wind. Some of these can still be seen.

It was in the 1870s that it was realised that winter navigation was possible along these coasts, and then came the railway, built with private money, followed by a harbour and road communication and the town really began to develop. By this time the mass emigration from all over Finland to the U.S.A., Canada and Australia was in full swing, and many a third and fourth generation American today can point to Hanko as the place from which his great-grandparents started their long trek to a freer existence as they saw it, away from the Russian-dominated duchy. Today's inhabitants of Hanko are more fortunate. They live in a free, democratically run land in a pleasant town which has grown into one of the most popular holiday resorts as well as being the only free port in Finland; a clean tidy little place which has the tremendous advantage of having three sides facing the sea so that one can always be within sound and sight of open water. I stayed at the Hotel Regatta, facing over a small bay and promontory where gulls swooped and small boys played on the strand, and by the time I had had lunch—an excellent and reasonably priced one—the skies had cleared and I was ready to explore further.

First I made my way back to the eastern harbour, for I wanted to see a little more of the facilities which make Hanko regatta one of the most famous in northern waters. It takes place each July, along with the tennis tournament, bridge week and 'Lie abed day', on the 27th of the month. The last is a noisy, happy carnival day when you can do anything but 'lie abed'! So for the whole of July the population is swollen to double, sometimes treble its normal size. It is estimated that about 1,500 yachts visit Hanko yearly and I would think that a goodly proportion of these come during regatta week. This is the time when the two yacht clubs come alive with dances, receptions, prize-giving, etc., but when I was there they half slumbered, one looking out across the eastern harbour and the other on Vastfordsvagen near Chapehamnen. The casino along by the Badstrand also seemed to be comatose in spite of its fearsome cannon on the forecourt, so I set off to the House of the Four Winds instead, intrigued as much by its name as anything else. I found it, set on the promontory at the very end of Manner-heimintie. (Helsinki is not alone in having a road named in honour of the Field-Marshal it seems, and this one is justified because it was the hero of Finland who owned this very pleasant building in the 1920s and gave it its evocative name. The Field-Marshal used to spend his summers in those days in his villa on the island of Stora Talholmen, but alas, that house was destroyed, like so many of those of his countrymen, during the Second World War.) The House of the Four Winds proved to be a delightful little restaurant, serving excellent coffee and the most superlative cream cakes. If I am to be accused of

15   *The Orthodox Church of St Mary, Lappeenranta*

remembering places by the food they serve, this one will come very high on the list. Replete, and regretful that my eyes were, as always, larger than my holding capacity, I again went exploring, this time across the peninsula towards the beaches at Silversand (*Hopearanta* in Finnish) where I had been told I would find a camping site. On the way though, I found something else, the Taktrom chapel, a baroque Gothic and originally Catholic church, built in the 1920s, which had miraculously survived the war. Nowadays, it is popular for weddings, mainly perhaps because of its excellent photographic possibilities, but it was another area close by which caught my eye. Not far from the chapel there is the Russian War Memorial, built only in 1960. It stands very close to the graves of over four hundred Russian soldiers who were killed in this area. How often in the holocausts which man directs against his brother man must people find their resting places far from the lands which they call home?

When I was talking to some people later that evening back in Hanko I asked if many English found their way to this corner. 'Not many,' they said. 'We get a lot of Germans and obviously many Swedes and Danes, but most of the British make straight for Helsinki from Turku.' And yet, I thought to myself, as I looked out across the tranquil waters of the bay before going to bed, they should come. At least, some of them. There are echoes of English naval history here in this backwater, for when the English and French fleets tried unsuccessfully to capture the fortresses on the islands and on the mainland at Hanko during the Crimean War it was at a time of change for England's future fighting men, when the navy was realising that its ships were going to have to be iron from then on. It is worth visiting the Fortress Museum at Hanko, just to get another small perspective of the same period.

I have a strong suspicion that Turku still looks upon itself as the capital of Finland, or at least that it thinks it ought to be. I get the same feeling of superiority that never fails to impress itself upon me when I visit Bergen instead of Oslo, or indeed Uppsala instead of Stockholm, probably for similar

16   Temple Church, Helsinki

reasons, for in each case the capital was moved mainly for political reasons, but the rejected cities continued to house much of the cultural life of the countries concerned. By virtue of its position Turku (Abo in Swedish) continues to keep its contacts, particularly with Sweden, and the majority of the citizens are Swedish-speaking. Under the centuries of Swedish rule, Turku developed from a small trading post on the river Aura (*turku* means 'trade') into the most important town in Finland, and eventually the capital. It wasn't until Finland became an autonomous duchy under Russian rule that in 1812 the administration and government were transferred to Helsinki (mainly so that St Petersburg could keep an eye on the tricky Finns) and Turku was allowed to slide back a little into the role of second, and now third city in Finland. But still, it has a dignity and a reserve which becomes its ancestry, and what is more it has a castle and a cathedral to prove its pedigree!

I must be one of the few English writers to have been at a wedding in Turku Cathedral. Mind you, I wasn't actually invited. I just happened to choose that particular time to visit the Cathedral, and once inside I couldn't exactly walk out again, it would have been so rude. So I stayed quietly at the back of the nave, while the very young blonde couple—he in his stiff best suit, and she in a short white dress and a tiny white veil—made their vows and walked down the aisle towards the altar. In a way it was rather wonderful, for it meant that the Cathedral was not just a history book but rather a living breathing part of today, fulfilling a useful place in an all too materialistic world. But after they had gone out into their world to face their future, I took a little time to look at the past which was left behind them.

There has been a church standing on or near the present site since the thirteenth century, and although there has been a lot of discussion upon the founding of the Cathedral it is universally thought that the stone vestry of the original merchants' chapel was incorporated into the new building. From the centre of the Cathedral one can see an old gable end in the wall of the present vestry and many believe that this must be the oldest wall in Finland today. Be that as it may, the work was originally begun by a Swedish bishop called Johannes, and the church was to be of the same impressive structure as those found in central Sweden at Sigtuna, Skokloster and Strangnas. But only a small part of the building had been completed, comprising the chancel and part of the main aisle, when in 1290, in the manner of clerics, Johannes was promoted to be Archbishop of Uppsala and his job at Turku was given over to the first Finnish incumbent called Maunu. Now, Maunu was closely concerned with the mendicant friars who had arrived at that time from the Baltic area, probably from Estonia, and were building St Olav's monastery about three-quarters of a mile away; he much preferred their type of building, so he abandoned Johannes' plans and put his own ideas into practice, with the result that the Cathedral is a combination of two styles, Estonian and Swedish. Could this, in its own way, have been an unconscious forerunner of the development of Finland along the twin paths it now follows with such success? It is an interesting hypothesis.

By 1318 the Cathedral had been burnt down by the Russians in one of the endless wars which raged across the country. This time the Cathedral was enlarged to its present size and the tower was added under the influence of the designs of the Hanseatic towns like Lübeck, Danzig and so forth. By the end of the Middle Ages there were no less than 43 altars in the Cathedral, and the side chapels contained the tombs of the various bishops. In later times military leaders from Sweden were also buried in the Cathedral, among them the famous Samuel Cockburn whose ancestors must have come to Sweden from Scotland; so a Scot, of sorts, lies in Turku, within its very heart. The only royal tomb is that of Karin Månsdotter, queen to Erik XIV of Sweden, son of Gustavus Wasa, and in fact she is the only 'royal' to be buried in Finland. Her tomb is exquisitely simple and stands in the northern side chapel.

But the troubles of the Cathedral were not over by the seventeenth century. In 1827 Turku suffered a disastrous fire, a constant hazard in the wooden towns of the period, and along with practically all the rest of the city the Cathedral was gutted. Today, thanks to extremely clever and careful restoration, it stands in all its former glory to make Turku the seat of the Archbishop of Finland. One final thing before you leave the building: take a look at the frescoes above the choir. They were painted by R. W. Ekman and portray the first baptism of the heathen Finns into Christianity by Bishop Henry, that same English Henry who came with King Erik of Sweden in 1157 and stayed on to be murdered, and finally to become the patron saint of Turku. Whether Bishop Henry was really 'first into Finland' with the fiery cross is still arguable, but it is a pleasant tradition in thought, and it does mean that Scotland and England are both represented in Turku Cathedral.

I joined the queues to go around Turku Castle on a hot Saturday afternoon, mainly because the shops were shut and I was frustrated in finishing my souvenir hunting. Normally, I hate following the herd like a lost lamb looking for its mother, but on this occasion I was so enchanted that I forgot the multitude until I struggled in vain to get shots of the courtyard without hordes of ice-cream-eating visitors. But that was later. It really is a rather delightful castle, because it has been completely restored to the stage where it must be almost exactly as it was in its heyday, but cleaner! and, as I trailed up the winding staircases, I was trying to imagine how the Tower of London would be without its centuries of grime. It isn't the same, yet it *is* the same in a way. I half expected to see Queen Elizabeth I coming round a corridor. It could easily have been so, for after all it was the same period of history and Erik XIV did make a bid for Elizabeth's hand and was turned down—yes, the same Erik whose wife Karin Månsdotter is buried in Turku Cathedral—getting lost in the maze of history? Let's start again, and this time at the beginning of the Castle's history.

It was founded as a fortress camp in the thirteenth century to protect the trading town of Turku, for at this time Finland was already part of the Kingdom of Sweden. Inevitably within a hundred years or so the building was enlarged to provide for the fact that the King of Sweden could be suitably housed (and suitably safe) within its walls should he choose to come on a tour of his kingdom. This meant housing the soldiery and the ladies of the court. There was a chapel too, and this was made available to everyone, even to the humbler mortals who lived in the huts outside the Castle walls. When Magnus Erikson, King of Sweden and Norway, lost his crown to Albert of Mecklenburg the castle was besieged by the said Albert and burned down, but it soon reappeared in even greater splendour, and by the end of the fifteenth century it was a popular spot with many a visiting monarch. Charles VII of Sweden for instance, who had been Karl Knuttsson Bonde until his elevation to the monarchy, and who had played as a boy within the shadow of the Castle when his father had been Commandant, visited it several times during his reign.

Its real heyday however, came a little later, after a very troubled period when the Castle changed hands between Danes and Swedes and back again. The Great Gustavus Wasa took his son Johannes (Duke John) to the Castle in 1555, spending the winter there, and, in the following summer, the Duke took up residence in the Castle with his Polish wife, Princess Catherine Jagellonica. Both of them were patrons of the arts, and the Castle received a facelift. They added a new storey, designed by a Swedish architect, which was placed above the medieval section and was furnished in the opulent Renaissance style so that the Duke and his wife could hold a brilliant court. But this too, was not destined to last. By 1563, Erik XIV, who was the Duke's brother, became jealous of the Duke and besieged and captured the Castle, sending the Duke and Princess to imprisonment in Sweden. (It was somewhere about this time that Erik was pressing suit to Elizabeth of England.) In 1570 Duke John had his revenge, dethroning Erik and imprisoning him in Turku from whence he went to another prison, to madness and death.

During the visit of Gustavus Adolphus in 1614 another great fire destroyed the castle and yet again it was rebuilt, but by now it was considered too out of date for habitation, and was relegated to becoming a store, leaving only the chapel to be used for its original purpose of worship. It stayed that way, becoming more and more decrepit, until the present century. Then it was decided to restore the building to its former glory, but the Second World War broke out and in 1941 there was still another fire, leaving just an empty ruin of the main building. But the Finns don't give up easily on anything, let alone the task of restoring a mere castle. After all, they were embarking on restoring a nation at about the same time. Work commenced in 1946, and, in spite of difficulties, cost and endless problems, the work was finally completed in 1961.

Now the castle is almost exactly as it must have been in Duke John's day, with its medieval apartments, the women's quarters and the Duke's own suite, but the Castle church was put back to as it was before the fire in the seventeenth century. It has been beautifully and most cleverly done, but perhaps the nicest thing about it is that it isn't just a monument to the past, in spite of the inclusion of the comprehensive Historical Museum. It is used by the people of Turku for all kinds of important occasions: banquets and concerts are held there and cleverly hidden modern kitchens can cope with the catering; one can even hire the rooms for a wedding and what bride could ask for a more romantic setting on her most important day? The idea is that Turku Castle should fulfil the function for which it was intended, forming a focal point for cultural and national occasions, and I must say that I found it very impressive. But I also couldn't help feeling that the present setup would, to coin a phrase, 'never have done for the Duke, Sir', but that perhaps is just because, for a fleeting moment, I thought I saw the couple in the wall painting in the East Tower frown a little at their Saturday visitors.

I had no such feeling in the Handicrafts Museum. This is another rather special place in Turku, for it was one of the very few parts of the town to escape the fire of 1827, that same fire which destroyed the interior of the Cathedral. The area was saved from complete extinction by its position on hilly ground. Hence the name, Luostarinmaki, which means Cloister Hill, and it was decided to keep the cottages and workshops intact so that generations to come could see how their ancestors lived and worked. The Museum is claimed to be unique in the northern countries, but there is a somewhat similar setup in Eskilstuna in Sweden. However, that is rather smaller and forms the centre of the old town, whereas Luostarinmaki is some distance from the centre of old Turku and only people of humble means came to live there, such as bricklayers, seamen, carpenters, etc. After the fire the remaining houses formed the nucleus of a new town, and more craftsmen came to the district so that by the end of the nineteenth century carriage-builders, shoemakers, tinsmiths, saddlers, and even a goldsmith set up shop there.

When it was decided to turn the area into a Handicrafts Museum to preserve it, all sorts of people came forward to help: tailors, bakers, furriers, glovers, and even though some of the crafts didn't have whole houses, they helped too, when rooms were to be furnished in a manner appropriate to their trades. For instance, a chimney sweep has one small room, while a ropemaker's tools are in view in a narrow lane. Nowadays, it is very difficult to find people who are able to carry on the old trades with the old tools, for many have been lost or forgotten, but still four or five skilled craftsmen work in the museum all summer and visitors are encouraged to try their hands too. In one shop I found the tobacconist was at work, hand-rolling cigars; in another, sweets and bread were made in the old ways; in yet another, I found a circlet of thick string which makes an ideal coffeepot stand, just as it did in days gone by. I use it daily, and my coffee stands upon it at this very moment. But one thing stays in my memory more than the craftsmen, the houses, even my circlet. As I came out of the door of one of the old houses into the afternoon sunshine there was a flurry of bright fur, and a small red squirrel dashed upwards into the safety of the eaves above my head, peeking at me for all the world like Mrs Bushytail. It was a reminder that nature is never far away in Finland.

With the wealth of background that Turku has there are, naturally, good museums, but two deserve special mention because of their unique qualities. Waino Aaltonen is surely one of the most illustrious names in the world of modern sculpture and design. He was born at Kaarina, just on the outskirts of Turku, and got his education in art partly at the School of Drawing of the Turku Art Association. Although there are many examples of his work throughout Finland, and there have been exhibitions overseas, there was no museum devoted entirely to his work, so it was in 1968 that the powers that be decided to build such a place. It is a spacious airy building, and one can see Aaltonen's work in almost perfect circumstances. Look for the young girl paddling—one can almost feel the chill of the water on her thighs, and see her diffidence. This piece has for me all the smooth beauty of line for which this sculptor was so lauded in his day, but it also has the strength that is obvious in much of his other work. The whole collection is a must for anyone interested in following the progress of art in this country where all forms of artistry are intermingled with the daily life of the land.

As with sculpture, so with music, particularly that of Sibelius, and so there is another pilgrimage to be made. It surprised me to find a museum concerned with Sibelius in Turku, for he was born in Hameenlinna in Hame province, but apparently he had relatives in Turku and many friends. One of these, a Professor Andersson at the university, started a collection of manuscripts of his work, and for a while they were all stored at the university. But then it was decided to house them properly and money was raised for the purpose. Apart from a very fine collection of musical instruments there are all the manuscripts and archives of every kind, including many critics' notices from first nights, and some of the notices are in English, so one is not completely cut off from knowledge of their content. Museums are not always my cup of tea, but I do believe that one should try to visit those which give a picture of the land which they serve because, quite naturally, they try to preserve the best and more unusual features, not to be found elsewhere.

With so many ferry connections between Sweden and Finland, many of them terminating in Turku, it is natural that this city should be the starting point for many tours, and among the increasing traffic of the past few years there have been many caravanners and campers. Few of them want to leave the archipelago without spending some time there, and the site that many make for is at Ruissalo, some 9 kilometres from Turku. It is a huge area stretching across several enormous fields. There are large parking areas, kiosks, a restaurant, toilet blocks and a barbecue, thoughtfully supplied with piles of chopped logs, sports areas and a sauna. While I am not particularly fond of such organised 'outdoors' it is good to be aware that such a facility exists within very easy reach of the ferry terminus. Hotels of course are fairly plentiful in Turku, but they do get booked up in summer months. If you want to stay in the centre of the town, among the best are the Marina Palace, Hamburger Bors and Seurahuone, but if, like me, you prefer a country setting, on the way to Ruissalo there is Ruissalo Hotel and further away still there is Raadelma Manor which has been converted into a hotel. Both these latter hotels have swimming pools.

Wherever you stay you should try to visit at least one or two of the old churches in the vicinity of Turku, because there is a lot of history hidden within their walls, which offers yet another aspect of the tangled web of Finland's past. Take Askainen for instance. This church is close to Louhisaari Manor, where Field-Marshal Mannerheim was born in 1867, and the manor has been closely connected with the fortunes of the church since they were both built in the seventeenth century. The door and the pulpit of the church were supposed to have been brought from Germany during the Thirty Years War by Finnish cavalry-men serving in the Swedish army. This possibly emphasises, if further emphasis is needed, that Finland's position under Swedish rule was not that of a serf, for within the church are the tombs of members of the powerful Fleming family, one of whose members was Klaus Fleming, Governor of Turku Castle. But pride of place is given to a brass chandelier which was donated by Field-Marshal Mannerheim when he visited Askainen in 1928, and it bears an inscription to mark the occasion. Louhisaari is now a museum and open to the public.

Nousainen church lies inland from Askainen on the other side of the main No 8 highway to Rauma. Tradition says that it is within a few kilometres of the spot where Bishop Henry, featured in the paintings in Turku Cathedral, was buried after his assassination. He was moved in the thirteenth century to Turku, but Nousainen is dedicated to the Saint, and as such holds a very special place in Christianity's march across the north.

If you come to Turku by ship from Sweden the chances are that your vessel will have passed by the Aland Islands, halfway between Sweden and Finland. You may even have been lucky enough to stop there for a while and watched the comings and goings at the busy little port of Mariehamn. If so, you will have noticed that all the conversation was being conducted in Swedish, and concluded that this was just because Aland comes into the Swedish-speaking part of Finland. That is only partly right, for in effect Aland is an autonomous province within Finland with its own elected government, but while the rest of Finland is officially a bilingual country using Finnish and Swedish, in the Aland Islands the only official language for the 22,000 inhabitants is Swedish.

Like the rest of this part of Scandinavia there were people living here in the Bronze Age, but indubitably the most important inhabitants of the 6,500 little islands, mostly connected by bridges, which form the Aland group were the Vikings, who opened up the trade routes from west to east, and for the archaeologist and historian Aland is crammed with interest. There are no less than six early ruined castles, nearly four hundred burial places with their mounds, and hundreds of house sites. Many of the grave mounds are near churches, so the conclusion is that even after Christianity came to the area the peasant traditions of burial continued and the churches were built on old cult sites. Like mainland Finland, Aland was part of Sweden for centuries until being surrendered to Russia after the Swedish–Russian War, and in the 1830s the Russians started to build the fortifications at Bomarsund. The building was unfinished when the Crimean War broke out, and in 1854 the fort was overrun by the French and English navies and destroyed. Hundreds of prisoners were taken and most of them, including some women and children, ended up in Lewes Gaol, Sussex, England. In spite of the fact that they were not harshly treated according to the manner of the times, conditions were certainly not good, and 28 of them died before release came in 1856. There is a monument to them at Lewes, erected by order of the Tsar Alexander II in 1877, which reads 'Erected by the Finlanders, Russian prisoners of War, memorial of their countrymen and fellow prisoners who died during their captivity in Lewes War Prison'. Nowadays all that remains to be seen at Bomarsund are a few ramparts, and the place of the fort has been taken over by a camping site and a café, but it can still be an evocative place for a British visitor with imagination.

When Finland became an independent nation in 1917 Aland became part of that nation, but it was to prove a point of issue between Finland and Sweden for four more years, until the matter was settled amicably through the League of Nations in 1921. The islands were awarded to Finland but became neutral territory. In the 1930s Finland proposed co-operation with Sweden for defence of the Aland Islands, but thanks partly to the criticism of the plan put forward by both Hitler and Stalin, Sweden rejected the idea and they still remained neutral. Today in spite of being officially part of Finland, yet having so many language and cultural ties with Sweden, Aland is very different to both of them. It is almost impossible to put a finger on why this is so. Perhaps it is due to its long traditions of seafaring, for Aland had impressive numbers of windjammers in the days of sail, traces of which can be seen aboard the four-masted museum ship *Pommern* moored in Mariehamn harbour. Perhaps it is due to the kinder climate of the summer Baltic waters, which allows many varieties of wild flowers to grow undisturbed and protected. But perhaps it is due to its very position as a 'bridge between the nations'—a bridge of water, traditions and cultures, that it has developed along its own lines, particularly in tourism. In summer many from both Sweden and Finland come to the islands, mostly on holiday, but also to take jobs at the hotels catering for visitors, while all year round there is a constant stream of Swedes who come to shop for food commodities which are cheaper in Finland than in Sweden. Also there is a slow increase in the number of foreign tourists who stop off for a few days in this most delightful archipelago, if for no other reason than to live in a summer cottage for a few days at a pace of life which exceedingly pleasant and increasingly rare. The real joy of Aland for me is in the freedom of the islands, the open spaces of the Baltic waters, the opportunity to live as one pleases.

Mariehamn, the 'capital' was founded in 1861 by Tsar Alexander II. It is a nice little town of about nine thousand souls, most of whom live in private houses, and it is very proud of its title of 'the town of a thousand lindens'. It has a museum or two including the aforesaid grain ship *Pommern*, the maritime and Aland history museums. One of the most interesting places is Kastelholm. Built to strengthen Swedish defences in the Baltic in the fourteenth century, the castle saw many battles before fire destroyed it in the eighteenth. Nowadays the remaining wing houses a Cultural Historical Museum and the nearby Jan Karsfarden farm gives an idea of life in past days in Aland. The Tourist Office will willingly arrange excursions.

Back on the mainland, Naantali is only about 10 miles from Turku, and is a small summer resort with a very popular beach. The town is made famous mainly because the president of Finland has his summer home 'Kultaranta' there (you cross the Ukko Pekka bridge to get to it and you are allowed into the park). It also lays claim to being one of the oldest towns in Finland because it was formed around the convent of St Birgitta, established by Bishop Magnus Tavast in 1438. The cloister of the church was intended for the use of both monks and nuns and Finland's oldest known author, Jons Budde, was in holy orders there. When the Reformation came to Sweden and Finland the cloister was closed in 1527 by order of Gustavus Wasa, but the religious were not evicted and the last sister lived there until her death in 1591. The buildings were then torn down, with the exception of the chapel. Inevitably there was a fire (1628), but some of the treasures were saved. When you visit the chapel look for the altar cloth, made by the nuns in the early part of the sixteenth century, and look too for the ordainment crown in the first vault. Both are very valuable and of great rarity, particularly in Scandinavia.

It was during one of my searches for good camping sites that I happened upon the Finnish Naval War Memorial. It stands in forest in Kuparivuori, on a hill between the sports stadium and the steep descent to the sea. It commemorates those who lost their lives during the Winter War and the Continuation War. How often in this fair and peace-loving land one finds echoes of the bitter past! They start out at one, like the headlines on a newspaper, and constantly remind that the peace is only of today, and we hope, with them, of tomorrow.

The small towns that string out along the coast of the Gulf of Bothnia are familiar to visitors from Norway and Sweden, for many have ferry links with towns on the eastern seaboard of Sweden with subsequent onward links into Norway. But they are not so well known to tourists from Britain or the Continent, although the more adventurous of these often find their way to Finland on these links, such as the Blue Way, via Mo i Rana and Umea or Sundsvoll, to Vaasa. The whole coastline is attractive with its small islands and the towns themselves have a distinctive way of life. Rauma for instance has always produced beautiful lace, and has a reputation for its fund of stories directed against the next town along the coast—not that a foreigner could understand them, because the dialect I am told is quite difficult even for a Finn to cope with. But apparently the good-humoured rivalry between Rauma and Pori has gone on for generations, somewhat in the manner of the constant cracks between Glasgow and Edinburgh.

Pori was built originally by Duke John (the one who lived in Turku Castle) in 1558 as a trading centre, and it has continued as one ever since. It has had its ups and downs including the inevitable fire, this time in 1852. Due to the fact that the land is slowly rising from the sea the town is now some 10 kilometres inland. Pori set up the first Finnish language theatre in 1872, and in more recent times has become the venue of the only jazz festival in Finland. This is held in July each year on Kirjurinluoto island in the Kokemaenjoki river. It has pleasant beaches close by and the best known of these is at Yteri, where the sand dunes stretch for several unspoiled kilometres. If you have a penchant for mausoleums, take a look at the Juselius one in Kappara Cemetery. It has a rather beautiful and delicate neo-Gothic design. Its architect was Josef Stenback. But its main feature is the restored frescoes by Gallen Kallela and Halonen. Painted originally between 1901 and 1903 it is one of the few pieces of Gallen Kallela's work to be found outside museum collections.

North of Pori, Kristinestad is a little town which claims to have the narrowest street in Finland. It is worth a stop in Nykarleby too, not because it claims to be the smallest town in the land, but because it has old wooden houses and there aren't many of them left, particularly after the Second World War. It also has close connections with Zachris Topelius who, with Runeberg, did so much to influence Finnish nationalistic feeling in the nineteenth century.

Roughly a hundred and fifty kilometres inland is the Ähtäri park, Finland's first wildlife preserve. It houses the animals which are indigenous to Finland such as wolves, lynx, beavers, reindeer, elk and even foxes, and also quite a number of birds. In these conservation-conscious days it is very necessary to give these creatures a chance to multiply and get back to their own living conditions. Finland, fortunately, has the room to do this, and the park will enable people to study the animals in a natural habitat from a watch tower. There are also plans for a hotel complex in the form of a hotel and wilderness cabins in the vicinity, and already the camping site is in use.

Inland Ostrobothnia is famous for other things too. During the days of the mass emigrations from Finland a vast number of the voyagers came from this area, and because they were a tough people, with an enormous capacity for drink and fighting, the Finn rather unfairly, but quite naturally, got a reputation which has stuck firmly abroad ever since, particularly among immigrant communities in the States, and it is only now that the image is tempered a little. Mind you, the Ostrobothnians were deserving of the label. Within the area, during the mid-part of the nineteenth century, gangs of ruffians used to terrorise the poor farmers who only asked to get on with their struggle to live. The Puukko gangs, as they were called, because of the wicked-looking *puukko* or knives that they carried (and didn't hesitate to use) were hard drinking, immensely strong men who arrived at markets or dances, or even weddings, beating up people, killing for the sheer pleasure of it, stealing livestock and even destroying the rooms of houses. It was said quite often that a wedding wasn't a real wedding in the district unless someone got killed in a *puukko* gang fight! It got to the stage when even the churches were not safe from them and finally a new sheriff, Adolf Hagglund, came to Kauhava, got really tough with them (at about the same time as the Revivalists started to appear in the province) and put most of the leaders behind bars, but just as in the Wild West a whole folklore grew up around these roughnecks, so that today all sorts of stories are told about their exploits and one is not certain how much is true. Today the area is calm, but they are still tough, these Ostrobothnians, but perhaps not quite in the same way. It is probably just as well.

Vaasa stands at the narrowest part of the Gulf of Bothnia, and again one can see how fast this part of the coastline has risen from the sea in the last few centuries, for the old town, originally the port, is several kilometres inland. Vaasa is the main town of southern Ostrobothnia and as such has quite a collection of the art of the area. This is housed in several museums, such as the Ostrobothnia, the Wasastjerna House and the Brage at Hietalahti with its seal-hunting equipment. But the most interesting thing to me about Vaasa in recent years is the fact that it became the 'White' capital during the War of Independence in 1918, and this event is commemorated in its coat of arms, which shows the Finnish Cross of Liberty. The countryside is very flat inland, very well cultivated now, but these flatlands were the scene of many a bloody battle against Swede or Russian in past times. Along the coast the scenery is beautiful in a stark way, and it is worth going out to the fishing village of Bjorbeby, on the islands, reached by road or boat, just to get the feeling of the splendid isolation of the camping sites and holiday cottages.

The holiday atmosphere of southern Ostrobothnia is quite something in its own right. There is little to do, and gradually one just falls into the pattern of idling and contemplating the sea, the stones, the patterns of light and wind upon the waters. It must be one of the easiest places in Finland in which to find oneself thinking almost as a Finn. I say almost, because it would take a lifetime to really assimilate sufficiently to become one of these complex yet uncomplicated people. One cannot hope to do it on one short visit. But it is a challenge to try, particularly here, where so much of the past seems still around one, and where the very nature of the landscape helps the process of understanding the mysticism, the romanticism and the nationalism of so many of the men who helped to mould the future of their emerging nation in the nineteenth century, in spite of the fact that it has almost become passé to admit now that it existed.

In these surroundings it comes as no surprise to find that Johan Ludwig Runeberg came from Pietarsaari, along this Swedish-speaking belt of the west coast, and it is interesting to note that both Runeberg and Topelius wrote and spoke in Swedish, thinking and acting as Finns. As we have already seen the reasons can be found in the centuries of Swedish influence, but surely it emphasises the unity of the nation whatever tongue is spoken, and too that languages are not important for themselves, but only as a method of communication and as a means of understanding thought processes. People matter. Runeberg's *Ballad of Ensign Stal*, comprising several pieces put together in a series, had a potent effect upon the awakening nationalists in the nineteenth century and some of it was written about a battle which took place at Orovainen in the province of Lapue, some sixty miles inland from Vaasa, on 14 July 1808. The day is still a local holiday. The combatants were Finns (fighting on

17   *Old houses in the open-air museum at Imatra*

18   *The 'Lament for Karelia'*
in Imatra Cemetery

the Swedish side) and the Russians. It appears that the Finns won the day, but were as usual on the losing side. The first poem in the series became the Finnish national anthem, sung for the first time at a students' festival in 1848. It was enough to bring down stricter Russian censorship upon the heads of the Finns, but not before it had been instrumental in awakening the seeds of liberalism as it had been intended to do. One can visit Runeberg's first school in Pietarsaari. It is a little cottage on Visabacken, and now naturally it is a tiny museum. If one's early days at school are, as today's educators claim, among the most important in the formation of a person's thought processes, surely this small place has a highly important niche in Finnish history.

Kokkola, a few kilometres to the north of Pietarsaari, has a memory of a different kind. There is an English boat house museum, and in it one finds an English naval pinnace captured during the Crimean War in 1854. Eight British seamen, together with their officer, died in the fight at Halkokari and they are buried in the Maria Cemetery.

The coast is fairly straight north of Kokkola, and apart from Raahe, founded in Queen Kristina's time by the then Governor-General, Per Brahe, in 1649, there is little of real note for a visitor until one gets to Oulu. Originally a port for the export of tar, Oulu is the biggest city in northern Finland, with its own university and many industries. It has developed considerably in the last few years, and much of its new look has come from the prolific genius of Alvar Aalto, and from being known for generations as the 'city of the tar merchants', it is now calling itself the 'white city of the north'. I have never seen Oulu in summertime, only in early spring, when the last of the snows were disappearing and the fields were that shabby brown that awaits the arrival of new green, so I cannot really do it justice here. But it has a delightful setting, sheltered by Hailuoto island. It also has its own open-air museum at Turkansaari, an island in the river Oulu, with houses and relics of the district, and at Kempele a wooden church survives from 1686 (a rare event as you will have gathered by now), where the wall paintings

19 Selling fish and potatoes at the harbour, Helsinki

are by Michael Topelius. I'd like to go back there some day, either in midsummer, or in time for the Northern Lights Car Rally held in November. To me the great attraction of the northern latitudes are the 'white nights' of summer or the *kaamos* of the winter. Perhaps I would think differently if I lived there, for then I suppose, like every other Finn I've ever met, I would get excited at the sign of the first green on the birch, or a little sad at the flame of autumn.

By no stretch of the imagination can Kemi be called a fantastically beautiful town, but it is an extremely important one. Like the other coastal towns its origins were as a trading post as long ago as the Middle Ages, but also it attracted fishermen to settle there because the Kemi river had an abundance of salmon. This fact is commemorated in the rather delightful salmon sculpture right outside the Merihovi hotel, where the three fish leap in the familiar curves so exciting to any would-be fisherman. The town is famous today for its timber-processing and its huge mills, and for the cardboard also made there. There is also one citizen who is rather forgotten. He is the Dean Rungius, whose mummified remains are rather ghoulishly on show in the medieval church! He's been there quite a long time, for he lived in the seventeenth century. Kemi is considered to be the border of Lapland. I mentioned elsewhere in this book that I once walked into Finland across the bridge at Tornio, from Haparanda on the Swedish side of the border. This has been the prerogative of many thousands of visitors, for the border has no customs and no guards and the inhabitants of both towns cross back and forth as they please. There is little to say about Tornio, but perhaps the bridge should be mentioned again, because it has a little history of its own. It was here in the First World War that many wounded soldiers and officers were exchanged, so that for some, at least, it was the end of despair and the beginning of hope. For me Tornio is and always will be the beginning of Lapland, and when I reach it my heart leaps with joy, but it is also the moment when one says goodbye to Ostrobothnia, and so, sometimes, the joy is tempered with regret.

6. Eastwards

'You don't know Finland until you have been in Karelia. I can't explain the difference, but you'll see it for yourself.' This was the comment of a girl-friend of mine one evening as we leaned over the balcony of her pleasant flat just outside Helsinki, watching the changing patterns on the waters of the Gulf of Finland, and her words were very much in my mind as my Finnair plane flew northwards towards Joenssu in the very heart of what is left of the fair province of northern Karelia under the Finnish flag. Below, there was a metallic glint on the vast waters of the lake systems, their reflective colours washed out by the brilliance of the early morning sun, so that the islands looked like footprints on silver-grey taffeta and the neat fields resembled green parquet, and, as we came in to land at the small, tidy airport, I was anxious to find out just what lay behind my friend's words.

That was my very first visit to the eastern districts of Finland, and I know now exactly why so many tough Finnish faces soften a little, and take on a faraway look when they speak of the provinces which border Soviet territory. To begin with, the countryside itself is very different from the rest of Finland. It actually has hills! One can stand upon them and see the panorama of forest and lake spreading below, without having to ascend a man-made tower to find a view. It isn't spectacular in the sense that Lapland or Norway can be, but it has a romance, a gentleness, a fragrance about it, as well as a surprising warmth in the summer months. It was far hotter on that first visit than anywhere else in Europe apart from the eastern Mediterranean, and I was extremely glad that I had learned the lessons of summer Finland before, and brought thin clothes with me.

But the winters are long, fierce and bitter, and the contrast perhaps has its part in the complexity and enchantment which is Karelia.

And still, it is only an infinitesimal part. It is the people who are Karelia and one cannot write on the eastern provinces without their appearing in large measure. They are the salt of Finland. This is natural, when one looks at the hardships, the endurance, the sufferings and the joys through which they have passed over the centuries. One cannot help but admire them, and in addition, one cannot help but like them for themselves. I have a feeling that this must show through as I attempt to write about the beautiful land in which they live, cramped now in comparison with the space that was originally theirs, but still large and gracious to everyone who has the good fortune to visit it.

Karelia supplies much of the legend and folklore of Finland. It was here that Elias Lönnrot spent so much time delving into the stories which now form the *Kalevala*. It was Karelia which inspired Runeberg to write some of the nationalistic poetry which was to influence much of Finnish thought in the nineteenth century. The beauty changes little despite the wars which have devastated the land throughout the centuries, for flowers and trees are a determined lot and grow regardless of man's attempts to destroy them. But it must have been far more difficult to trace the origins of the folktales, for there was no written record of these and Lönnrot was reliant almost completely on the willingness of people to sit down with him and recall the stories told to them in their youth. Perhaps though, it might not have been quite so difficult as first sight would indicate, for these, the people of Karelia, are not so reserved as the rest of Finland. Watching them at work and play, in various places and under various conditions, I have been struck time and time again by their flashes of almost Latin temperament. The hands gesticulate, the eyes flash, and the laughter comes spontaneously. I am inclined to believe that there is a great deal of truth in the maxim that 'to be able to laugh, one must first learn how to cry'.

Karelia has certainly had her tears. I was reminded forcibly
of this when I visited the small war cemetery in Imatra once,
and saw the exquisite memorial which guards the place. It is
the statue of a woman, her head bent in sorrow, yet in every
line of that figure is pride and dignity. They call it 'Lament for
Karelia'.

There was no lament when I spent Midsummer Eve in a small
country community just north of Liperi. Quite the reverse! I
had been invited to attend the celebration so that I could know
for myself just what it was like to attend a gathering of country
people on one of the most important nights of the year. I had
been asked to be there about nine in the evening, so I climbed
into my car in very good time and started off in the general
direction I had been given. What I hadn't been given and
should have remembered to get was the exact location of the
place I was looking for. And there was just no-one to ask:
everyone goes to ground at Midsummer. No sign of life at the
scattered farms, no cars on the roads. No-one even at the occasional house or sauna. It was a completely deserted countryside through which I was travelling, and what's more there
seemed to have been some sort of conspiracy to take down all
road signs, so I spent almost two hours looking for Kompere.
It never did appear on any map or sign and the fact that I
found it at all was entirely due to good luck, my instinctive
bump of direction and a refusal to believe that it didn't exist.
Kompere proved to be a tiny group of museum houses tucked
away beside a fast running river on the side of a little country
lane, and I only found it because, on turning a bend in the road,
I suddenly saw people. I found my contact looking anxiously
for me, and she introduced me to an upright old gentleman in a
neat black suit and trilby hat, who was the absolute twin of a
dearly beloved old friend in Norway. When I got to know him
better, I told Mr Johannes Heikonen, for that was his name,
that he had a double of his own age in Norway and he wasn't
a bit surprised. He just smiled and said that he and his family
came originally from northern Finland near the border, but he
had 'met and married a nice lady from Karelia so had settled

here fifty years ago'. This is the third person I've met in Scandinavia—one in Iceland, one in Norway and one in Finland—who were so alike in looks and ways that they could have been brothers. Surely this tends to prove that the ties of kinship between the people of the north are very strong?

Old Johannes took me first into the dark interior of one of the small museum buildings so that I could sign his precious visitors book and look at some of the little treasures garnered from all corners of the district. There was a cradle from the eighteenth century, farm implements—all of them clumsy heavy wooden things of immense strength—kettles and flat irons, linen chests and a really fascinating collection of old coins, most of them from Tsarist days. This little museum belongs entirely to the community and it must have taken a long patient time to put all these things so lovingly together. I liked it better than many a more sophisticated collection and would advise you to stop and look for yourselves if you are in the district. You won't get lost! Follow the main road between Joenssu and Kuopio and turn off after about an hour towards Liperi. It is easy now that I know how. . .

The entire museum is grouped as the old farms were, round four sides of a square, but this square was filled with people, benches, trestle tables heaped with heavy doughnuts and coffee urns and Karelian pastries, and all eyes were turned towards a platform where a fiddler was playing traditional tunes which lilted across the evening air. As he ceased and almost before the applause, another man leapt on to the platform to give a recitation, which, judging from the gestures and the eyes and the roars of appreciative laughter, must have been rather Rabelaisian in content. I think Johannes was quite glad I didn't understand, though I regretted it. But even my Finnish guide and interpreter didn't understand—she said the dialect was different to hers, a mere 30 miles away, so I was consoled. Then, the accordionist started up with a gay jig and people joined him on the platform, whirling and turning, some in summer dresses and open-necked shirts, others in national costumes, but all with a smiling familiarity with the music and each other and all the while the sun shone, sinking gently towards its midnight horizon, the mosquitoes buzzed around heads and ankles, and there was a frequent passing of bottles among the men, an inevitable accompaniment to any festivity, not just in Karelia, but everywhere in Finland.

I felt a gentle tug on my arm. 'Come,' said Meka, 'Johannes wants to show you the bonfire before it is lit, and that will be soon.' We made our way towards the edge of the river, where the huge bonfire had been stacked, and on looking closely I saw that it was mainly composed of old boats, halved and turned with the keels outwards. I asked whether there were any pagan superstitions attached to the building of a bonfire in this manner. 'No,' they said. 'The boats are no longer safe, so it is better to burn them.' The ever practical Finn; but perhaps this part of the origin of the expression 'to burn one's boats' (Finnish version). I did ask, but could never find out. Maybe that someone who reads this will enlighten me eventually. The bonfires themselves come, as elsewhere in the world, from the days when fires warned the populace of threatened invasions. Now it is only tourists who invade, and in this part of Finland there are very few of them.

Suddenly the bonfire crackled its warning to us and people crowded round to watch, hushed now as the fire licked hungrily at the boats. A small rowing boat was safely far out on the river, and I shouted to the oarsman to take me with him. He nodded and pulled in so that I could leap aboard, clutching my cameras for dear life, and, as he rowed out again into the fast-running central stream, I was able to see and to photograph the upturned faces, apricot coloured in the firelight against the backcloth of tall trees silhouetted on the sunlit midnight sky, while the haunting sounds of a pipe floated across the water towards me . . . just one of the myriad fires all over Finland on Midsummer Eve. For the past few years private bonfires have been forbidden in many places because of the lack of water in summer and the genuine risk of fire, so these public bonfires have become much more popular. For the visitor to Finland this is rather pleasant for he can join in such festivities to a

greater extent. The private parties naturally do continue to
have pride of place, but often they have to content themselves
with a barbecue beside the sauna instead of the former large
beach bonfires unless the year has had plenty of rain. Most
visitors can, nowadays, find a party of the type I was attending
by the simple process of asking the Tourist Office where the
public festivities are going to be in any given district. The rest
will follow, much in the way that I have described here. On this
particular St Hans Night I had had an invitation to a private
party as well, and had intended to go, but as I arrived back in
Joenssu at about 2 a.m. had thought it too late to put in an
appearance (the party at Kompere had still been going strong
when I left). Next day I learned that my friends had still
expected me. I shall know next time.

Joenssu is a pleasant town, set beside the Pielisjoki River. Its
main industries are connected with timber, and the memorial
on the river bank depicting two loggers, armed with the familiar
sticks with which they move and work the logs with amazing
agility, is one of the most familiar sights of the town. On the
opposite bank is a double-headed Russian eagle which commemorates the visit of the Tsar in the days of Russian rule. In
those days much of the shipping sailed through the Sainaa Canal
to St Petersburg and even on to the North Sea. In recent years
the canal was closed, but now that it has been opened with the
agreement of the Russians it may increase the traffic again
through this part of the lake system. There is a museum near
the loggers memorial, and there is also a very nice outdoor one
on an island in the river, but apart from these and the outdoor
theatre, when it has performances, there is little for the tourist.
One feature of all these small towns in Finland is noticeable at
once to people from countries which do not have metres of snow
each with monotonous regularity, and that is the condition
of the pavements. A surface seldom exists as we know it in
Britain, so one has a certain amount of rough walking even in
town. It's worth remembering this when walking around these
smaller towns. Use your sightseeing shoes, not town ones.

One afternoon I did find what to me is one of the gems of

Joenssu. This is the tiny Orthodox Church, typical of so many all over Karelia. It was deserted when I went in and I was able to stay for a long time, looking at its exquisite ikons and enjoying the tranquillity. These ikons preach the message of the Gospels and stem from the days when people were unable to read, but could follow picture messages, but they are not worshipped as images. All of the ikons in Joenssu Church were painted in St Petersburg (Leningrad). The oblique cross which one sees in Orthodox churches is interesting, for the cross bar symbolises the two robbers at Golgotha. The part pointing to Heaven represents the robber who acknowledged Jesus and to whom the promise of paradise was given. The downward bar represents the robber who blasphemed.

Easter is the main festival for the Orthodox Church, and to emphasise the Resurrection the church at Joenssu is white, to represent the Light of the World. I knew that I could not go into the area of the church beyond the ikonostasis, or screen, for only priests are allowed there, but I was looking at this ikonostasis when the door of the church opened quietly to admit the verger, and he opened the screen door so that I could see the altar from where I stood. He was able to explain to me that this church had been one of the fortunate ones for it had a large congregation now, largely drawn from Karelians who had come to Joenssu after leaving their homes in the east when the land was ceded to the U.S.S.R., and in addition to this building there is a chapel in the country at Petravaara. He also told me that the church was dedicated to St Nicholas, the same man that we know as Father Christmas.

The Orthodox religion is strong in Karelia for it was brought there from the State of Novgorod, the original Russia, and its colour and distinctive forms of worship appealed to the lively temperaments of the Karelians. Although nowadays it is, apart from the great Uspenki Cathedral in Helsinki, mainly confined to what is left of Karelia, with only little branches elsewhere in Finland (for instance the Skolt Lapp village in Lapland), it is very much a religion of the people. It is joyous, as anyone who has ever seen the *pradznik* festivals will confirm. The *pradznik* (the word comes from Russia) is the name day of a saint, and of the church consecrated to that saint, so that each year each church or *Tsasouna* has its own festival. After the two services, one in the evening of the day prior to the festival and one on the day itself, there are processions, carrying the holy images to the cemetery. But after that the merrymaking begins, and there is dancing, singing and feasting in which all are invited to join, and at which the priest himself is always present, for he is an essential part of the community, well loved and well respected, and the religion is a tolerant one. Orthodox priests are not required to be celibate, and many of them are married. The best *pradznik* for the visitor is the one held at Hattu Vaara, near Iilomantsi, in the only *tchasouna* (one sees this word spelt both ways) built in the time of the Russian rule of Finland that is still on Finnish soil. One can get a room in a village house, or live in a tent, for there are no hotels, but it is well worth the effort and is a wonderfully moving and memorable experience. It is gay, exciting, exotic, and yet so completely natural. What other religion has all that? Before I left the Joenssu church the verger pressed a slender beeswax candle, made by the nuns, into my hand. 'To remember us,' he said. I shall.

I had another surprise in Joenssu of a different kind. The Kaukonens, whose daughter is a friend of mine in Helsinki, had very kindly asked me out to dinner one evening. I was duly collected from my Summer Hotel Elli (which incidentally was really comfortable and spotlessly clean, *and* reasonable in cost) by a taxi, for again, 'no driving a car if one was to drink a glass of wine with dinner', and we pulled up outside a seemingly dead building in Siltakatu called 'Siltavuori'. Inside, and up in a lift, to find a restaurant with dancing, casino and bars, all in full swing. It is always amazing how Finland wakes up at night and yet all is hidden behind closed doors. One never finds this Finland unless told it exists.

Our superb dinner was taken in a delightful private room, elegantly set with Finnish china and cutlery, but the *pièce de résistance* for me was the bowl of delicate wild heartsease used as the table centrepiece. Only in Scandinavia does one find this use of wild flowers in homes and restaurants, only in countries who prize the coming of spring and respect the bounty of nature. It always makes me realise that we, in Britain, are far too profligate with our natural resources. It was the same when we went home for coffee to the Kaukonens' tasteful flat overlooking Pielisjoki River. The coffee table, set with silver and fine china, had a vase of humble clover and buttercups, and they looked more exquisite than the finest orchids. I had forgotten how lovely they were, and it took me back to the days when my small daughter used to bring them from the fields at home, and, for a moment, I felt very homesick.

I had a couple of hours to spare one afternoon when staying in Joenssu, and decided to go out along the Lakes in search of a beach, instead of using the very good swimming pools in the town. There are several beaches to the south, along Lake Pyasela, particularly where the camping sites are, but I was selfish enough to want one to myself. I headed towards Kontio-lahti, plunging off the main road at the Auuro turn towards the lakeside, but somehow I missed the narrow turn to the beach and landed up beside a military barracks and a most spectacular piece of sculpture. It was a great spearhead, made of glittering black stone, and inscribed across its base the dates 30.11.1939–13.3.1940, and the words *Kolla—Koski*. A memorial to the Winter War, set in the middle of the forest land for which that war was fought so bravely and bitterly. This land of Karelia has so many memories.

There is little bitterness today. At least, not on the surface. But when one talks to people who came from the districts which are now in Soviet territory there is still a longing, a nostalgia and a resentment. Practically everyone I came in contact with in Karelia was a member of a family which had come from the old districts. The young, whose mothers and fathers had come. The middle-aged, who had come themselves as children and teen-agers and whose parents had had to leave a lifetime's work behind them. The old, whose farms were left before the harvest was gathered, whose animals were slaughtered or driven before them, who turned their backs on everything they held precious because they prized freedom of speech even more. I asked many if they had gone back, for they can cross to visit and are allowed into the old districts with little difficulty placed in their way. Some had been back. Others shook their heads, for they didn't want to see the changes which they had heard about from those who had been. 'Our homes are here now,' they said. 'And we are lucky. We have kept our identity and our communities, and we live in a democratic land. We live.' And, after all that is the best memorial of all. I went for my swim in the clear lake with a quiet heart after leaving the memorial to Kollà.

A hundred kilometres slightly northeast of Joenssu is Iilomantsi, one of the few places in Finland where battlefields of the Second World War can be seen on the Finnish side of the present border. I do not think that the Winter War can ever be overestimated by people outside Finland, for it was partly the fierce resistance of a handful of Finns against the might of Russia which caused Adolf Hitler to underestimate the u.s.s.r. sufficiently to open a front against her instead of concentrating on annihilating the west. Oinassalmi is on the left-hand side of the road just before reaching the bridge across the river. There is a modest monument and, behind it, hidden among the trees and the rocks, there is an old trench. Much of it has fallen in now, but it has an evocative power for those of us who are old enough to remember and respect. When I was there the ground was smothered by wild *kiello*, lily of the valley, which is Finland's national flower. I thought that was most appropriate.

It was just a few kilometres more into the beautiful Petkeljärvi National Park, so I took the dusty road into the area to find the pretty camping site, perfectly situated as usual by the deep green waters of the lake, but plagued by mosquitoes. It is no wonder that Finns love birch trees. They use them for sauna, for shade and shelter, and for mosquito switches, flapping the leaves enthusiastically about their persons as if still in the sauna. It works up to a point, but then the mosquitoes divebomb under the leaves, and even I get bitten in Karelia.

There are other things to be seen at Iilomantsi, including a

Karelian house, built almost in the style of the old ones, now alas, no more. There is a restaurant in this one, but I was surprised and not a little annoyed to find that one was expected to pay a mark to enter, whether having coffee or not, and there wasn't all that much to see. The outside is really the best part, for when I was there the surrounding garden was ablaze with golden yellow flowers which on inspection proved to be dandelions and they looked magnificent. This was yet another example of nature being allowed her say too. The interior decorations of the house *are* attractive and genuine, and the coffee good, and it is the only café for quite a long way . . . so perhaps it was worth the mark after all.

That evening when I got back to Joenssu I was invited by the mother of the young guide who had conducted me around on Midsummer Eve at Kompero to partake of some rather special Karelian food, for Mrs Taijala was one of those whose family had left Karelia when she was a young girl, but she had kept alive many of the traditions of Inpilahti, from where she came. Finnish people are rather nice in this way, and this family in particular. I had been unable to get breakfast before a very early start one morning and so coffee was ready for me at this house, together with sandwiches, because, they said, 'You cannot possibly go off with nothing. It is too long a day.' These are the things that are remembered long after the reasons for them are gone. On this occasion I was to partake of *sultsina* and *keitinpiirakka*. We sat in the gaily painted kitchen and got the food piping hot from the stove, and it was marvellous. Meka said proudly that her mother made these two dishes better than anyone else and I could well believe it. *Sultsina* is a very thin crispy pancake filled with a kind of rice pudding, and when I said in Helsinki that I had tasted this, I was told that many people in Finland didn't even know it still existed, though it was made sometimes for tourists at a special feast. I didn't ask for the recipe: this is something that has to be tasted in a certain place at a certain time. Nothing else would do. *Keitinpiirakka* is again a kind of pancake, filled with whole dry cooked rice and eaten with a butter and hardboiled egg paste. The dish used to be given by a girl to her fiancée in the old Karelian traditions, and the main reason for my being served with this was that on the morrow I was to go to see a representation of a Karelian country wedding in the old style, and Mrs Taijala wanted me to get off on the right foot! I certainly did that.

Before I left that evening the Taijalas presented me with a length of pure linen, made by Mrs Taijala, and for which she had collected the flax, spun it, and then woven it. It is the same type of linen from which men's shirts used to be made years ago in the districts just north of Lake Ladoga. One day I might make it into a skirt, but now I prefer to look at it in the piece and marvel at the patience which made it and many pieces like it over the years. You can find handwoven linen still in Finland, for the art is very much alive. Many women make their own materials, and though it is rather expensive it is very lovely and wears for ever.

Due to the fierce winters in this eastern province, it was customary in the days before the advent of the motor-car and reasonable roads for all social events to take place in the summer months, when the whole district would receive invitations to the celebrations, and weddings of course were no exception to this. Nowadays weddings take place all the year round like anywhere else, but the local Tourist Board have hit upon the idea of making a special representation of the old Karelian wedding so that traditions may be kept alive, and too in the hope that it will attract more visitors to their area. I was to attend one of these in the district of Saarivaara, about two hours' drive eastwards from Joenssu, right on the Russian border. It was impressed upon me that this was only the second year that it had been tried out, and that all the action was performed by people of the district. Again the weather was unbelievably perfect as Meka and I drove through the glorious countryside heavy with leaf and lilac blossom, to find another young guide who was to narrate the action for the wedding. We found her house without difficulty, which was rather an achievement in itself as all the information we had was that she lived near the library. I think she was rather startled to see us so early in the morning. However, with customary Finnish courtesy she hid her surprise, took out her rollers and offered us coffee. We still had quite a long journey through deep forests and across rolling farms before we got to the place chosen for the performance, and on the way we came to the no-man's land of the border area with the U.S.S.R. There is a youth hostel right on the edge of this no-man's land with an excellent view of the two lookout towers, one Russian, one Finnish, but one is not allowed to photograph, so *don't* take your camera out of its case. However, it was worth seeing and the youth hostel is worth remembering as a good place to stay in this remote and almost forgotten little corner of Finland. As one might imagine, there were other holiday-makers there already. Some Finns, two Dutch, and two German, who also had come for the wedding.

The performance was to take place in a bowl formed by the hills backed by a birch wood, and facing some of the loveliest countryside in all Finland. The stage consisted of a representation of an old Karelian house divided into several rooms, with one wall open to the audience and a small apron stage built out from it. Further up the hill there was another small stage, and this represented the *tchasouna*, and apparently this had been blessed so that it was holy ground so that the priests could perform the wedding and it would be a legal one. 'But this is only a play,' I said. 'Oh yes,' came the answer, 'but for the ceremony we take the actors out and put in a couple who want to be married and then we can have a real wedding! Nobody sees the difference!'

The audience were to sit on long wooden benches, spaced up the hillside which formed the auditorium. I was introduced to the stage bride, already dressed in her old-fashioned grey woollen gown, with her hair braided into plaits, who sat in full view of the audience on the uncurtained stage licking an ice-cream cornet, while other members of the cast helped with last minute touches to the set or fiddled with their wigs. The order of battle was to be as follows:

The main festival of the wedding takes place in the bride's home to which the bridegroom and his best man would come in horse-drawn carts (I could hear the horses snickering and stamping somewhere within the spinney at the back of the stage, so they too were ready for the 'off'). Within the house an old woman would bring bread and *kalakukko* to the table and the mother of the bride and her helpers would serve coffee to the guests and make speeches to which the old men would reply. In former times this was the moment when the dowry gifts were brought out, because, as in all peasant communities, marriages were often an arranged affair as part of a business alliance. While all this was going on the bride was to be seen in the next room preparing to take sauna with her friends before the ceremonial dressing, and before the token weeping by the old ladies to protest at the loss of a daughter from the house. Then the bride's brothers would bring the bride to a chair where other men removed the ribbons from her hair in readiness for cutting. From the time of marriage a woman wore a linen hat called a *tzepsy* and her hair was never shown in public again, so it was cut short at the wedding. After the bride received her parents' blessing, which consisted of holding bread above her head, she was presented to her groom. The wedding breakfast would come *before* the wedding and would consist of Karelian hotpot, and at this stage in the play there would be an interval. That would give time for the real couple and the priest to arrive, for the real ceremony in the open *tchasouna*. After that, the play would continue for the speechifying, the dancing, the reception and the general jollifications. It looked more and more like a long ordeal, not only for the cast but for me too if the play was to be in Finnish—and country Finnish at that!

By now the wooden seats were nearly full as more and more cars assembled in the field below the open auditorium. I hadn't seen so many cars in one place since leaving Helsinki. But along with the audience and the refreshments laid out on trestle tables at the top of the hill, came the mosquitoes, and everybody was flapping birch trees round their heads until it was more like Birnam Wood coming to Dunsinane than a wedding ceremony. The fiddlers and accordionists started to play, the cast took their positions, the bride polished off the last of her ice-cream and the

20   *A representation of an old Karelian wedding, Saarivaaria*

21   *Karelian beauty in national and modern dress*

reluctant horses drawing the wedding carts came galloping round the bushes to the front of the stage.

I have rarely been so entertained. It was splendid. Everything was so delightfully natural. The cast had one microphone between them, which they passed from hand to hand, frequently getting tangled up in the flex and strangling each other in the process, but never ever forgetting words or being put off by anything, for the action of the play continued, completely ignoring sundry small boys from the audience who climbed up on the stage and explored the set with not one word of reproach from actors or audience (Finns believe in giving children freedom of action; I longed to take them by the ear and throw them out). Dancers danced, singers sang, the family greeted their visitors with a deal of '*Terve, terve*'—'welcome, welcome' —and a lot of back slapping, the audience slapped even more fervently at the mosquitoes, and then, to cap it all, the clouds came up and it began to rain. We were not to be daunted: up went the umbrellas, out came the rolled-up raincoats.

The clouds cleared away and the sun came out again. Then the bride's hair was taken from its braids and the symbolism began to take on its real meaning as the bridal pair clambered into the cart that was to take them to the wedding, but instead of going up to the little chapel they disappeared appropriately enough into the bushes. Interval. We all stretched our cramped nether regions and made for the waiting coffee urns in the farmyard, and I saw that two priests of the Orthodox Church had joined us. So the real wedding was not so far away. We managed to get ice-cream and some Karjalan *piirakka*, yet another form of pastry. No wonder the Karelians have problems with waistlines. 'You were quite right,' I said to Meka, 'your mother makes better pastries,' and she beamed happily. We were prevented from further conversation by the arrival of a bearded little man who was introduced to me as the local bard, one Petter Mantaisen by name, who is something of a one man *Kalevala* in his own right because he writes in the old style. He struck a pose for me, offered to sell me his book of verses, we shook hands and then the word got around that the wedding was

22 The scene from the viewing tower at Kuopio

about to take place, so the entire audience legged it over to the
tchasouna to get vantage points around it.

It was during the time that the real couple arrived to take
their places in front of the saffron and gold robed priests that I
felt that we had no real right to be there. This was no play.
These were youngsters who were making their vows for life, she,
dressed in a simple printed summer minidress, and he resplen-
dent in his best suit, accompanied by their respective parents
and friends, and here we all were, making a Roman holiday of
it. But I couldn't go away. It was too fascinating as the pair held
their candles and made their responses while the crowns were
held crookedly above their heads, and we all held our breath. I
stole a look at the bride's mother. A tear glistened at the corner
of her eye. The bridesmaid wept unashamedly. I wanted to cry
too, but I kept on photographing. Then I realised that I had
been wrong to feel that we were intruding. This boy and girl
were having a wedding that they would remember all their
lives, in front of a bigger congregation than they could ever have
expected to attend, and there was only one thing missing. To
make it quite perfect, at least for us, the bride and groom
should have been given the opportunity, if they wished, to dress
in national costume, so that their wedding would have been
even more a part of the lovely land in which they will make their
home.

Meka and I left while the dancing was in full swing. We had
a long journey back to Joenssu and it was getting late. The day
had been a long one, but to me it was something I shall remember always, midges, rain and all. The Tourist Office says that
the villagers hope to put on this performance twice each summer
from now on. Do go to see it when you go to Finland. It will
enchant you, just as it did me.

Koli is about two hours' driving northwards from Joenssu,
and is one of the most picturesque places in Karelia because of
its hilly setting. It is also one of the best-known holiday venues,
with a magnificent cottage complex complete with its own
restaurants, beaches and two saunas (log and smoke) as well as
a super modern hotel which perches right on the top of the hill

beside the skilift and commands one of the finest views in Finland.

Lomakoli—'Holiday Koli' in English—was opened in 1968, and the wooden cottages nestle in the trees right beside a small lake called Karankalampi which is much warmer for swimming than the bigger inland sea of Pielinen, part of the great Lake Saimaa system. The cottages are most comfortable, simply but fully equipped, as all these holiday cottages in Finland are, to enable a family to look after themselves for meals if they don't want to go into the central restaurant. The saunas are on the beach at Pielinen, about ten minutes' walk away. I was looking forward to my spell in the smoke sauna. There is no doubt that the acridly sweet smell of the smoke adds to the unmistakable feeling of wellbeing and that a smoke sauna is able to be taken hotter without feeling the effects. The clear cold waters of Pielinen felt wonderful after the sauna, and I swam for a very long time before going to dress and eat lunch, refreshed, relaxed and with a skin which felt like the satin of the lake waters. I wish I could have a smoke sauna in my own garden in England, but without the Finnish lake it might not have the same effect.

The Touristhotell at the top of the hill is modern, smart, always busy and rather on the expensive side, but immense fun to visit. It is entirely different to its holiday cousin by the lakeside, but each complements the other, and it is rather nice to be able to have a change of view by getting into the chair lift and going up, or down, for the evening, if you don't want to take the car up the winding road. My companion shut her eyes firmly when we sat in the chairs, and clutched the poles for support. Finns aren't used to heights. They take their risks in different form.

From Koli one can take a ferry across to Lieksa, where the main attraction is the open air museum, an impressive collection of houses and their contents from all over Karelia, and, from Lieksa, as from many of these towns, you can take a bus to the border area. These Finns are used to living close to the big brother next door, but foreigners are not quite so blasé and find the experience impressive. There is constant traffic back and forth across the borders by Finns who go to work in the u.s.s.r. on various contracts, and occasionally there is some excitement when a Finn falls in love with a Russian girl and tries to smuggle her with him. Sometimes he succeeds, but more often they are caught and she must stay behind. Life is not kind to Romeo and Juliet, even today. One seldom meets Finns who say that they are not glad to get back into their own free air. Here in Karelia, one can get many excursions into the Soviet Union, but there must be some preparation with visas, etc., and these are better arranged from Britain beforehand. I had made no such preparation, so I was happy just to stay in Koli, enjoying the clean air of the pine forests and sleeping the sleep of the just when the birds and the morning sunshine (at 2 a.m.) would allow it, and just talking to the many Finns on holiday who, like me, find that the Finns of this part of Finland are much more like Russians than other Finns, both in build and I think in temperament. The humour is dry, sharp, sometimes sardonic, and often downright Rabelaisian. Perhaps that is why it appeals so much to a visiting Briton, even in translation, and why western and Helsinki Finns enjoy the change so much.

Kuopio is about 390 kilometres from Helsinki. It is a very pleasant run by car, but a long one, so once again I caught the ubiquitous Finnair domestic flight network northwards to save time. The local flights have so many interchange points at the most surprising and seemingly out of the way places, so that nowhere is more than a few hours from Helsinki. I do not know of such a comprehensive system anywhere else in Europe. The airways have become the transport of the people as the pioneers intended them to be, and a lot of people just turn up at the airports in Finland in the same way as they wait for a bus or a train elsewhere. For this reason it is wise, if a visitor, to book several days in advance.

My main reason for going to Kuopio on this occasion was to visit the Orthodox Museum there, the only one of its kind in western Europe, and the repository for many of the most precious treasures of the Finnish Orthodox community. Without seeing it I felt that I couldn't possibly grasp the intensity of the feeling of Karelia, nor could I hope to understand just why the community has survived so well. The trouble was that I arrived on a Monday. Nobody had thought to tell me that the Museum was shut on Mondays . . . however, a telephone call or two from the ever-obliging Tourist Office to explain my presence and I was on my way accompanied by an English-speaking guide who looked amazingly like Nana Mouskouri. It didn't surprise me at all to find that she was a Greek from Athens who had come to Finland with her medical student husband while he worked on a research project.

We were met at the door of the museum by a sweet-faced slender woman who turned out to be the wife of the priest-in-charge, and who spoke good but unpractised English. She led us into the maze of rooms, unlocking the doors before me and explaining the exhibits and their history as we went.

The Orthodox faith has remained firmly entrenched in Finland for many hundreds of years despite ups and downs in its fortunes. It was in the eleventh century that the missionary Saint Sergius was told by the people of the district, 'We are simple folk. Our wise men live on the island of Valamo. Go there and talk with them about your Faith,' and it was then that the monastery of Valamo, on an island in Lake Ladoga, came into being. Over three hundred years later in 1393 St Arsenius, so the story says, 'set out in a small boat leaving himself to the Will of God'. A storm blew him to the island of Konevitsa, and so another monastery was born. In the time between these two happenings the Roman Catholic Bishop Thomas instigated a Holy War with Novgorod, the original fount of the Orthodox religion, to try and convert Karelia to Catholicism, but then it was Prince Alexander of Novgorod who stood firm, and he is still given a day to himself every 30 August. The Church had a lot of problems during the many wars between Sweden and Russia, but after the Treaty of Nystad in 1721, when large parts of Finland were ceded by Sweden to Russia, Peter the Great set about reviving the Orthodox faith and by the end of the nineteenth century services were being conducted in Finnish. During the period of

the Grand Duchy, under the last of the Tsars, Russian arch-
bishops were put in charge of the Finnish Orthodox Church and
the Russian language was taught in the Church schools. It
wasn't until after the declaration of Finland's independence in
1917 that the Church resumed its original form and it was
transferred from the Patriarchate of Russia in 1923.

The Winter War and the Continuation War again brought
troubles, for most of the members of the Finnish Orthodox
Church lived in Karelia and it was to be Karelian territory
which had to be ceded to the U.S.S.R. under the peace treaties.
Almost the entire population moved westward rather than be
left under Soviet rule, and with them moved the monks, taking
their precious regalia, relics and treasures with them. The
humble people removed their beloved icons and crosses from
the parish churches too and brought them, with paintings and
altar cloths, to a new life safely within the borders of the
redrawn Finland, often sacrificing many personal possessions
to carry the treasures. All too many had already been lost or
destroyed in the fighting, but some have come from the villages
and townships of Viipuri, Kakisalmi, Korpiselka, Suistamo and
many more. One can imagine how terribly difficult it must have
been in that bitter weather, struggling to get the heavy loads
across the ice, particularly from Valamo and Konevitsa, but
determined people can do anything, particularly when faith
moves them.

A lot of Karelians settled in Helsinki, becoming members of
the congregation of Helsinki's Uspenki Cathedral. Some went
to other districts of Finland, for at one stroke it was necessary
for western Finns to share their farms, often splitting them in
two with the refugees. But a large number stayed within north
and south Karelia, swelling the numbers of the congregations of
the many churches which had not been disturbed, like the ones
in Joenssu and Iilomantsi, so it was decided that the headquarters of the Archbishop should be situated in Kuopio, also
a centre for many Orthodox members, and a residence was
built for him there. Then there was the question of what to do
with the magnificent treasures that the people and the monks

had brought with them. Some would, quite naturally, go to the new monasteries built along the shores of the lakes to house the communities of Valamo and Konevitsa, but it was felt that many should be able to be seen by everybody, and not locked away, and the first Orthodox Church Museum in Kuopio was opened in 1957, removing to its present building in 1969. Some of the older priests express the hope that one day the monasteries will be reorganised and the treasures go back to their original owners, but even if this reorganisation should happen, many of the items are so priceless that the risk of their destruction by careless usage would be unthinkable, and so the present premises are the very best place in which they can be housed. One cannot help but have a feeling of reverence for the beauty that is before one's eyes in each room and in a way they do much more good to the soul of man by being seen by over thirty thousand people each year.

Almost the first thing that greets the eyes in the main hall of the Museum is the icon of the Holy Face, which came from the church in Kakisalmi, and, in a way, it sets the feeling for the rest. One is almost overwhelmed by the wave of reverence which permeates the building. This is hardly a museum in the normal sense, but an extension of the church itself. It is as tranquil as the church at Joenssu, and as happy. And how can one choose which items are the most beautiful or the most out-standing? Surely the beauty must be in the eye of the beholder. There is the stark simplicity of the bark bow and crucifix, probably made, and most certainly used, by St Arseny, even though the crucifix is now imprisoned in a gilded frame. There is the cool magnificence of the pearl-studded icon of our Lady of Konevitsa and the gleaming silver cenotaph of St Arseny (who, incidentally, received his training at Mount Athos in northern Greece); there are the exquisite modern iconostases, taken with priests when they had to travel far across the country-side to see parishioners; chalices, tabernacles, crucifixes in profusion. There are the agonising penance chains, made of iron and worn in secret by the ascetics of Valamo, the huge tomb of St Sergius and St Herman, the opulence of the covers made for this same cenotaph and the delicacy of the 'made without hands' icon which, legend tells us, is the same as the imprint found on the Holy Shroud, and, most moving of all to my eyes, the humbler icons of St Laurence and St Alexei which came from the chapel at Raimala. Parts of them had to be sawn off by the villagers to fit them into their boxes for safe keeping when the war came. There in this mutilation is the desperation and determination of Karelia. Some of the most interesting historical exhibits are the pictures and sketches of the monasteries and hermitages as they were over a century ago, for these give a very clear idea of how the islands looked then. I have it on good authority that these monasteries are now used as homes for old people. Under the circumstances, perhaps that is the very best use that can be made of them.

I have no idea how long I spent at the Orthodox Museum, but it was a very long visit, and before leaving I was privileged to be taken into one room which is not open to the public, though one can see it through the glass door panel. This is the private chapel, used by the priests when they come for seminars and training. It is very much like any other Orthodox chapel— composed, calm and much decorated. But there are two features which make it outstanding: one is that the icons were painted for this chapel by a Japanese and on examination one sees that all the facial features are Oriental; the other was a silver-framed icon, lying by itself on a plain stand. This had been brought only a week or so before by the head of the Orthodox Church in Russia, when he came from Moscow to visit Kuopio. It is possible that in this single item lies the greatest hope for the future that the Museum has.

The centre of Kuopio is unremarkable except for two things. Its statue of the original Kuopion Man, called 'Brother' and sometimes irreverently referred to as a town councillor, and the Market Square. Kuopio Market is famous throughout Finland for its flowers, for its colourful Romanies and for its *kalakukko*, the pastries filled with pork and small fish from Lake Saimaa, called *muikku*. We know this fish as vendace, or whitefish, and it is rather like a small sardine. I intended to buy one of these pastries from the many stalls offering them, but decided that it was rather on the big side to buy a whole one, so I'd settle for sampling it in a restaurant. Locals claim that one hasn't been to Kuopio without tasting *kalakukko*. I hate to admit it, but I don't think one misses much in the years of abstinence. . . Dinner, taken in an intimate little tavern tucked away in an arcade, was much better. There are a number of hotels and restaurants in Kuopio, even a pub which is not bad for an imitation of the real thing, but many people make their rendezvous now in a new motel called Iso-Valkeinen, where the food is good and there is dancing each evening. This is a facet of Finnish life that I find very pleasant, for it doesn't start until quite late, in the manner of Spain and Greece rather than the north, and it suits my mode of existence. I was staying at Iso-Valkeinen, and it was pleasant to be able to walk by the lakeside en route back to my room, which was comfortable and exceedingly modern. So modern in fact that it wasn't until next morning that I discovered the television hidden inside the table. Television isn't bad in Finland: there are always so many imports from Britain, the u.s.a., Germany and France that one can understand most of the offerings and it is interesting to see local and Iron Curtain features too.

Kuopio's most popular time of the year is during the Dance Festival in early June, when performers come from all over the world to compete. If you intend to be there about that time, book your accommodation well beforehand.

One mustn't leave Kuopio without mentioning the Tower, pride and joy of the local populace. Puijo was the first revolving tower of its kind in Scandinavia. It is 75 metres high but it stands on a hill, so that the observation platform is about 224 metres above sea level and the views are superb on a fine day. It boasts a café, a restaurant and, at the foot of the tower, beside the skilift, there is a small lodge where one can sometimes get accommodation of a modest kind, particularly popular too, as a winter café.

Kuopio is the terminus for one of the Lake Saimaa steamer routes. There are many of these scattered over the vast region of lakes and canals and one spends hours getting from A to B. The fussy little boats bear the names of the towns to which they travel—*Savonlinna, Imatra, Kuopio, Lapeenranta, Pukaharju* and *Heinavesi*—and their passengers come from all corners of the earth. On *Heinavesi* one day there were a doctor and his wife from Australia, two girls from New Zealand, a student opera singer from London, two Israelis, a Scots family complete with kilts, several Dutch and half a dozen Germans, and in the middle of them, one elderly pint-sized English lady. This was in addition to a couple of dozen Finns and myself, and naturally, the 'crew' which consisted, as far as I could count, of an assortment of kitchen and bar hands, one engineer, the captain and his mate, who seemed to combine the jobs of ticket collector, multilingual guide, steersman and deckhand. He was a slim grey-eyed young man of about 27 who said he'd been doing this job for several summers now and enjoyed every moment. 'I think this is one of the most beautiful places in the world,' he said as we stood surveying the calm waters. I didn't like to ask how much of the world he had seen, but in any case I was prepared to agree with him. These lakes are beautiful, and it doesn't matter what the weather conditions are like, they have a dress to suit. The boats only run in the summer months, because during winter the lakes are completely frozen over to a depth of several feet, and as elsewhere in Finland, that is the time when boats are laid up and cars and sledges take their place as the transport of the Saimaa system.

The Captain of the *Heinavesi* was small, wrinkled and about 60 years of age, and had obviously spent many of those years travelling the lake. 'You are lucky to be travelling with us and with him,' said the guide proudly. 'He is the most experienced of all the captains and knows everything of the waters.' Certainly the way in which he brought his craft into the landing stages betokened a familiarity with the vagaries of winds and weather. We tied up and cast off as fast as a London bus. But there the resemblance ended. There could be nothing less alike than London Transport and this delightfully cumbersome creature with the genteel atmosphere of yesterday. There is a small

dining room forward, which copes adequately with two full
sittings of hungry passengers and serves substantial, tasty meals,
beers, coffees and cakes from a minute but spotless kitchen.
There are some day cabins for those who want to have some
privacy from which to gaze on the panorama of lake and
islands, a lounge and a miniature covered deck aft. I had hoped
for sunshine, but I was glad of my anorak as I settled myself
in a deckchair beside other hardy mortals and watched the
black and green satinned water changing behind us into moiré
taffeta, rustling like an old lady's many skirts.

The journey from Kuopio to Savonlinna lasts ten hours. The
lock systems take time to negotiate in spite of the fact that
nowadays most of them are operated by electronic computer
systems from smart new cabins beside the locks. No longer is
there one old man turning a wheel by hand, but still the
processes are fascinating and more than one passenger climbed
off to have a closer look and was so entranced that he had to
jump for the boat as she was pulling away. A goodly number of
these passengers already knew each other because they were
travelling on the same package tour, which included the lake
cruise. They had been to Lapland and to Helsinki, to Turku and
Jyvaskyla and were now returning to Helsinki again, all in nine
days. I asked one what he thought of it. 'Don't reckon much,'
he said. 'Nothing to see. Not a very interesting country.' I ask
you, how can you hope to see very much if you are working on
a principle of 'If it's Tuesday it must be Saimaa?' Every
country needs a little longer than that, and Finland demands it,
for so much of the interest is hidden from the cursory glance.
The package tour passengers got off the steamer at Heinavesi
as they were to visit the convent at Lintula and the monastery
at Papinniemi, and it was my turn to regret that I had no time
to go too on this visit but, before they left, one Australian made
an interesting comment about Sibelius, whose music, so she
told me, was the reason for travelling half across the world to
see his native land. 'I haven't been a bit disappointed. It is just
like his music. He is supposed to have based much of it on the
swooping movement of two great birds in flight, and here in

Finland, one feels that movement in the winds.' I thought that was one of the most perceptive remarks I'd ever heard about the man, his music or his country.

For those who want to spend their holidays on and around Lake Saimaa, visiting innumerable small islands, there is a rather interesting scheme operated by a Savonlinna Travel Agency. They call it Lake Adventure, and it offers camping, fishing, swimming, sauna, boat travel, all with an accompanying guide, who helps with the preparation of the meals. One of these fine Finnish summers, I might try that . . .

On this occasion, my journey's end was to be Savonlinna, one of the more interesting and lively towns in the Savo district, and also one of the oldest, for it was founded in 1639 and has seen much of the history of Finland battled around it. Because of its position it was always a meeting and trading place and, inevitably, at the centre of disputes between Sweden and Novgorod as to the exact placing of the border of Finland for nearly 600 years.

It was because of this, and because the Cossacks were continually making raiding sorties into the area inhabited by Finns, that the Constable of Viipuri Castle, one Erik Axelsson Tott, commenced in 1475 to build a fortification which would discourage them. He called it after Olav, King of Norway, who had by then become a saint, and in 1639 Savonlinna was given a town charter by Per Brahe, Governor of Finland at that time. Even so, the border line swayed back and forth behind and ahead of it, so that for half of the eighteenth century the area was Russian territory, but when Russia finally took over Finland from Sweden, Savonlinna and the eastern parts of the country came back into what was to be called the Grand Duchy of Finland; it was when Saimaa Canal connected the lakes with the Gulf of Finland that the town really started to develop around the Castle, for the great timber rafts used this route. After the Second World War the canal was shut, but the new canal is open now and Savonlinna is increasing in importance, mainly because of the huge mechanical wood-processing factories which are established there.

Savonlinna's main attraction for the tourist lies in the castle which dominates the town and which is also the venue each year for the Opera Festival. In Tsarist days the Russian aristocracy were attracted by Savonlinna and its spa—diplomats, army officers and their wives used to spend their summers boating and picnicking during the long days and enjoying the gaiety of the soft evenings at the Spa Hotel, the Casino or in their villas. The old Spa Hotel was burned down in 1964 and a modern luxury hotel appeared in 1968, but the Casino is still there and functions as a summer restaurant. Quite close by is Knut Posse, a students' hostel which makes another excellent summer hotel during the vacations, and there are also still some of the old Tsarist villas in use on Casino Island, so there is a variety of accommodation if one includes the other good hotels like Tott, Suerahuone, etc. It was late in the evening when I arrived in the town, and I was vaguely irritated at being told that I was to stay in the Annexe to the Spa Hotel, particularly when I learned that it was about 10 miles from Savonlinna by road, though only 3 miles by boat. The passion for understatement isn't the prerogative of the English. The Finns have it in large measure. I should have realised that I hadn't got the whole story as I set out for Rauhalinna.

At the end of the nineteenth century a Finnish general in the Tsarist Army, Nils Henrik Weckmann, decided to build a hunting lodge in his favourite Savo district. He had been absent from Finland for many years and some of that time had been spent in the Crimea, so he built his dream home in the Byzantine style he liked so much from that area. Rauhalinna was the result, and when I saw it I was completely enchanted. It is a small white wedding cake of a building, surmounted by fairytale turrets, standing on a cleared knoll, and reached by a long and bumpy drive through acres of black forests, through which one gets an occasional wink from the lake. The residential car park is behind the hotel and when I stepped into the narrow hall, my case was seized by a smiling little waitress in a long red dress who started up the uncarpeted wooden stairs with me in pursuit. I found myself on a longish balcony, running like a ledge above the high-ceilinged dining room, decorated in pink and yellow and white icing, and sporting a huge ceramic ovened fireplace which could have graced a Chekhov play. My room led off this balcony, and it too possessed one of these enormous fireplaces, as well as magnificent stained-glass windows. The room was rather small, and my guess was that originally this must have been a dressing room for one of the master rooms; this was borne out by a later look at the rooms on the other side of the landing which had once comprised the suite for the lady of the house. My only complaint was that one had to share a bathroom, and I was unlucky enough to have a German couple as neighbours who seemed to spend the entire night and day in the bathroom, so I hied myself along the 'ledge' to another one, fervently hoping I didn't meet another guest—or the house ghost—on the way.

The General's rooms downstairs lead from the restaurant, and a small door in the wall was pointed out to me—'for entertaining people privately'—another masterpiece of under-statement. The poor man didn't get very long to entertain any-body at Rauhalinna after his retirement for he died within two years, and the property changed hands several times, the original furniture disappeared, and now only the mirrors, the fireplaces and the decoration are as they were in his day.

During the Winter War and the Continuation War the house became the headquarters for the secret services of the Finnish Army, and after the cessation of hostilities it served as a holiday home for NCOs and their wives. It belongs to the Finnish State Museums Department, and was restored by them to its present exquisite state before being leased to Spa Hotels who are now responsible for its maintenance. I dined in a small anteroom completely decorated in opulent Turkish style, where wall-papers and fireplace are so new-looking that I thought they were recently installed, but they were built in with the house and are completely original, having been brought from St Petersburg. I half expected a dashing Cossack to throw open the door, hand on hip, to survey us with a haughty glance, and I wasn't entirely disappointed, for in came a family of nine swarthy Romanies in the brilliance of pink, yellow and red satin, favoured by the gypsies of Finland, to sit in the main dining room for coffee and soft drinks, so there was an exoticism, even if of a different kind, below the painted Italianate frescoes.

There is also supposed to be a ghost in the outbuildings of the house, but it didn't materialise while I was there. Perhaps it was because the nights were so light. Even the birds were fooled, for they were singing their hearts out at midnight, and then, as they stilled, another shift took over. A nightingale serenaded from a tree close by for over two hours before the day birds, suitably rested, took up the morning chorus as it spilled across the silent rose-coloured waters of the lake. Such is the enchantment of the white nights . . .

While staying at Rauhalinna, I took the opportunity to visit Kerimake to see the largest wooden church in the world. It was built to house a congregation of three thousand people from all over the scattered parish, originally including Punkaharju and Savonranta. Seen from a distance it is quite impressive because it is painted, like Rauhalinna, to resemble stonework, and when one gets inside it is interesting to see that the same effect was attempted with some success. It is now undergoing restoration to bring it back to its former glory and there is to be a central heating system, something not included in the original estimates. I went round the church with a girl who had spent her childhood in the village, and she told me that the great building had never been used in winter except at Christmas. 'Then,' she said, 'we put on all the clothes we could find.' Near the church is a small fishing jetty with a handful of tiny red huts, and a few boats tied alongside looking over the vast expanse of inland sea and sky that one finds everywhere in Finland, and where the elements merge into each other and into infinity. It is extremely difficult to capture such moments with a camera, but the challenge is impossible to resist if you are a keen photographer and you will find yourself halted time and time again, saying, 'Well, let's try,' and often being gratified and surprised at the resultant beauty. So, when travelling in Finland on your own itinerary make some allowance for moments like these. They have a habit of eating time away.

I had to put a spurt on to keep an appointment I had made to meet someone at the Hotel Finlandia, out at Punkaharju ridge. This is one of the loveliest holiday areas in the Savo region. Formed in the Ice Age, the ridge connects Lake Puruvesi and Pihlavesi and is dotted with camp sites and holiday villages around waters so clear and clean that one can drink from any of them. The camps are so cunningly concealed in the forests that one never sees them and so the area stays, outwardly at least, completely unspoiled. Runeberg, Finland's national poet, came to Punkaharju and there is a monument on the side of the road, bearing a few lines of the poem he wrote to commemorate the occasion. There are some hotels in this area too, like the Finlandia, set far into the woods some 28 kilometres from Savonlinna on its own beach. The Finlandia was once a leave centre for officers of the Russian army, so the building is an old one still bearing the Tsarist crest. The present owners have been sensible enough to keep the furnishings and atmosphere completely in keeping with the building so that a 'lost world' atmosphere envelops one from the moment of arrival, but there are today's dances in the evening, excellent food and all modern conveniences, and many people, particularly from Germany, like the Finlandia enough to book from year to year.

Another appointment I had was of a very different kind. I had been asking the lively Tourist Officer, Perrti Mutka, about the history of Olavlinna, Savonlinna's fortress, and during the course of that conversation I asked how the fortress had been provisioned. He told me that most of the food had come from farms quite close to the castle and that some of these farms still existed, although of course their role today was quite different. There the matter had rested, but a day or so later he telephoned me to say that he had arranged for me to visit one of these farms and meet the owners, so after breakfasting one morning in the sleepily baronial atmosphere of Rauhalinna's breakfast room, I went to Tykkylanjoki, just a few kilometres away on the road into Savonlinna.

I turned off into a narrow lane which brought me into the main square of the farm buildings, built in the typical style seen in so many museum collections all over Finland and Sweden, but this was a living, working place, and the people who met me at the door of their home were the descendants of a line of owner farmers, not nine-to-five caretakers. I was ushered into a cool dark hall made gay with flowers and *ryjy* rugs and onwards to a large lounge from which a sun porch overlooked the peaceful fields towards the lake. Reuina and Ann Ikonen have lived and worked at Tykkylanjoki all their married life. They told me the farm was built over two hundred years ago, but it came into the possession of their family in 1890. The ceiling of the lounge was done in silk, which was part of the original decorations, as were some of the wallpapers in the house. I asked Mrs Ikonen how she managed to keep it clean. She laughed: 'Thank heaven for vacuum cleaners.' She took me into the vast kitchen with its huge fireplace with a platform on top 'where people slept in the winter in the old days', she said. In another corner of the kitchen was a huge loom with some work in it, for like many Finnish women, Mrs Ikonen finds time to do her own weaving. She pointed out to me the fireplace in the dining room. This is a special treasure, because it is exactly like the one at Hvitrask, and was designed by Saarinen. It was rather nice to see this in a real home and in use, because these are museum pieces in Finland today. Finally we went into Mr Ikonen's study and for a moment I was really back in Grand Duchy days, for all the terribly heavy leather and wooden furniture had come from Old Russia and it was as though a page from a history book had sprung to life. This is a feeling one often gets in these eastern provinces of Finland in spite of their modernity.

'I must visit Olavlinna today.' I made this resolution one sunny morning after idling on the jetty at Rauhalinna, following that delightful occupation known as 'watching other people work'. So off again past the farms with the fat cattle and the hay pikes, along the lake shore and the deserted main roads, back to Savonlinna.

When Danish-born Eric Axelsson Tott chose a rocky island in the fast-running sound of Kyronsalmi for the site of the new fortress he chose wisely, for it is a splendid vantage point, and although the castle of Olavlinna has changed masters at various times in its chequered history, it was two hundred and fifty years after its building before it fell into enemy hands for the first time in 1714. At the time of the Opera Festival a pontoon bridge is built across the narrow sound from Tallisaari park, but at all other times the approach is by ferry and one sounds a bell for the boatman. Usually one can get a guided tour around the castle after using this regular ferry, but once more I had chosen an unfortunate time to visit, because it was closed to the public for a few days while being prepared for the Opera Festival, and it was only thanks to the good offices of Perrti Mutka that I was able to get in at all.

When the rowing boat came for me I was surprised to see that it was manned, or rather womanned, by a sturdy, bespectacled elderly woman with arms like tree trunks, who waved us impatiently into her craft while holding it expertly with one oar against the insistent stream and muttering imprecations the while at a small outboard motorboat parked in what was evidently considered to be 'her' place; as we cast off from the bank she gave the offending boat a hearty swipe across the engine for good measure. While pulling us across the sound to her stronghold, she chattered away in a flat Savo dialect which was all but incomprehensible to my companions from other parts of Finland, but apparently it was to the effect that the stream was never frozen not even in winter, that other boats shouldn't be at the landing stage, and she always got the job of ferrying people across because the boatman was never there. On arrival at the landing stage below the castle wall, she leisurely got to her flat slippered feet, heaved herself ashore, tied up the painter, and allowed us into 'her' castle.

This was my introduction to Olavlinna and to the redoubt-able caretaker of that fortress. Heta Korhonen, who will for ever be Heta Olavlinna in my mind, is one of the characters of Savo. She has been looking after Olavlinna for 35 years and knows every stick and stone of the place, and provided one gets her at the right moment and with a competent interpreter, she is a mine of information. Otherwise one must make do with lesser mortals or with a guide book. I asked her what she was going to do when it came to retirement to be answered with 'Voi Voi', and the statement that she had a small flat in Savonlinna, but there was no question of giving up for a long time. I also asked rather humbly if she had considered having a motor for her little boat to make it easier on her and the answer was a decisive shake of the head and the comment that oars were much easier to handle. Perhaps she is right, the way she handles them. She told us to go where we liked but to take care where we walked, and, if we got lost, to go to any window and shout and she would come and find us. Then she disappeared into her own fastnesses and we were left to our devices, and obediently set off.

It is much bigger than one thinks from the outside. The remaining towers are joined by sentry walks and curtain walls and these surround deep courtyards seldom reached by the sun's rays. Through an archway one reaches the Great Courtyard, which was littered with the impedimenta for tiered seats and staging for the festival. The walls and outside staircases form a large and impressive set, and, as I walked into the shadows of the arches I was confronted by a dragon's head and the petrified trees of the *Magic Flute*, so that the castle began to take on a dream quality and one could almost hear the music reverberating against the uncaring stones. As we ventured into the interior of the castle and within the towers we soon discovered the reason for Heta's warning: there were winding staircases leading to rooms in every direction and we had a job to keep track of each other, and when we tried calling within the walls to find out where the long circling stone corridors led, and if they returned to the same places (they never did) our voices came back flatly to us. I found my way up an ancient staircase to the top of the former Bell Tower where I could see out of a narrow archer's slit towards the blue and orange tents of the Kyriniemi camp site among the trees across the rippling water, and thought that it must have been like that for the castle's defenders when they saw the camps of their attackers over the centuries.

It is no wonder that a dozen legends have grown up around Olavlinna, two of which are particularly attractive.

St Olav, after whom the castle is named, has his name day on 29 July each year and in medieval times it was customary for the first lamb to be born in spring to be called the Lamb of St Olav, and to be sacrificed to him and eaten in feast. It is probable that a black ram was always reared in the castle for this purpose, so the saying 'to live like the castle ram' grew to mean that some-one was very well fed. However, there appeared a significant entry in the Church Register of Saaminki in 1728. It read, 'Nothing of note has happened except that the last ram of Olavlinna fell into Kyronsalmi Sound from the battlements and was drowned.' There is a rather nice statue of Olavlinna's ram in Tallisaari park—he looks distinctly annoyed.

The other story concerns a rowan tree which until very recently used to grow from a crevice just below the parapet of the rampart in the small courtyard. It was said that its red berries grew from the heartblood of a maiden who had been immured alive in the wall. There are several versions of why she was there: one is that she was condemned for treason, but was innocent; another says that she was hidden from the enemy but that the only people who knew she was there were killed in the battle.

A final little quote from a book written in exile by a Swedish historian, Olaus Magnus, and published in Rome in 1555. It says:

In a remote part of northerly Finland there stands a castle belonging to the Kingdom of Sweden. It is called New Castle and it has been built with extraordinary ingenuity and fortified both by human skill and by Nature. The castle being situated on a round hill, it has only one entrance and exit on the western side. By order of the guards of the King of Sweden or the feudal lords residing in the castle, a raft fastened to the gateway by thick chains is laboriously drawn by means of pulleys across the river every night to prevent the castle being attacked from the shore [authors note: no Heta!]. An unusually broad, immeasurably deep river starting in the White Lake flows past the castle. Its bed is black, especially round the castle, where all the fish are also black. In the event that a Governor of the castle dies suddenly or a careless guard condemned to death for neglecting his duty or sleeping at his post, is hurled from the highest battlements in accordance with the laws of the castle, a fairy playing a guitar rises from the waves, thus foreboding some misfortune as seen above.

I was roused from my reverie by a call from the others and descended the endless stairs to the courtyard where Heta was waiting. She said that she thought I might be interested to see something and led us back into another part of the castle not previously probed by us. The thick walls have held their share of secrets over the centuries, but now it seemed that they were to be the repository of new ones, for we came into the most modern and beautiful kitchens. These are being installed while the restoration of Olavlinna is being undertaken in order to offer a complete catering service for receptions, congresses, conventions, etc., in the castle, in the same way that Turku already does. It was very interesting to see how the complete installation is being done without disturbing anything of the original castle. By the time this book comes into print the rooms of Olavlinna may well be in regular use after their years of decay, providing unique and beautiful settings for the ordinary people of Savonlinna and the district over which its walls have brooded for so many centuries.

As we came ashore in Tallisaari across the bridge, past the salmon catchment where the fat fish *do* look black in the water and one is strongly tempted to try to 'guddle', my eye fell on a monument I had missed before. It comprised three massive natural rocks and is a memorial to the men who fell at Kollaa in the Winter War. How often those years slip unobtrusively into one's consciousness here on the eastern side of Finland . . . I took a moment to go to the 1918 War of Independence memorial too. It is by Waino Aaltonen and is erected in the grounds of the rebuilt Cathedral. After all, the past, present and future are all Finland. One is quite impossible to contemplate without the other two.

For anyone who has little time to spare in Savonlinna and has not already been able to take a trip on the lakes of Finland, there are excellent little tours which start from the passenger harbour beside the colourful marketplace. *Salmetar* takes 96 passengers and operates one-hour and three-hour trips with commentaries in various languages including English. At least you can get some idea of the lakes, the environs of the town, and of the might of Olavlinna from water level.

I drove down through the peaceful countryside from Savonlinna towards Imatra and had the road to myself nearly all of the way. At one spot a red fox carefully surveyed the road before crossing. His training obviously wasn't all that good, because he narrowly missed coming to a sticky end under my wheels. This is a pretty road, mostly forests, but the lakeside views were constantly changing and the fields were heavy with a harvest ready for the pikes. Also one is aware that the u.s.s.r. border is only a matter of yards away, but this is just a part of living for south Karelians. At Imatra for instance, there is a crossing place, and many Finns go daily to work within the u.s.s.r. on special projects. I went up as far as the no-man's land which separates the two countries. It is a different border to the ones further north because of this constant flow of working traffic and even in these sophisticated days there is something sad about the fact that without special papers one cannot just 'pop across'. The dream of travelling without visas and that passports should only be necessary to help in times of trouble is still far from realisation. Perhaps that is why I enjoy travelling within Scandinavia—these enlightened countries have at least accomplished that dream as far as they are able.

I found a really good restaurant in Imatra. It is upstairs in a baker's and confectioner's shop called Buttendorfs. I chose it because the shop looked so appetising and I needed a coffee and sandwich, but I ended by eating superb salmon and coffee-cake and it wasn't so expensive by Finnish standards. Keep it in mind if you are in Imatra.

An industrial town of some importance, particularly when it comes to wood-processing, electrical power and iron works, Imatra also has one or two rather special offerings which should not be missed by the tourist. One of these is, rather fortuitously, the Valtionhotelli, the only hotel of size in the town. The first tourist of any importance in this area was Catherine II of Russia who spent a lot of time and money in the place, attracted no doubt, like everyone else, by the magnificence of the Vuoksi rapids, but it was only in 1830 that a hotel of any importance was built on the west bank of the river, and this became the 'in place' for most visitors to Russian-dominated Finland in the summer season. Alexandre Dumas came there, so did Richard Wagner. And of course, so did members of the Russian aristocracy as well as well-known Finns. Inevitably there was a fire. But the new building rose from the ashes of the old like a phoenix and became even more fashionable, and it is this building which still exists in part today. It was visited several times by Tsar Nicholas, and there is a 'Tsar's room' to mark that fact. In the War of Independence it was a military hospital and in the Second World War was under bombardment and artillery fire. Today it has a more peaceful existence but one again gets the feeling of yesterday in the high-ceilinged rooms and the collection of armour and fowling pieces on its walls. It also has a lot of pictures depicting how the Falls used to be— thanks to the hydro-electric scheme bare rocks line the river bed and though until the end of 1973 the falls were opened for half an hour each Sunday, the power cannot be spared now to allow even that, so that the great river is probably lost for ever. Such is progress. On the opposite bank from Valtion-hotelli is a pleasant park and if you look carefully among the rocks you will find quite a few 'devils churns' from the Ice Age, formed at the same time as Saussupelka ridge, and made by the swirling violent waters. Across the road and beyond the bridge is a fountain with a rather strange piece of sculpture called the 'maid of Imatra' by Taisto Marikskainen. It is supposed to symbolise a girl who threw herself into the falls because of a betrayed love. All that today's Imatra maidens would get if they attempted the same end would be a broken leg or at best a severe headache.

Along the banks of the Vuoksi near the smart, black-windowed Town Hall there is a nice little open-air museum with old houses and a remarkable little collection of farm implements. I saw some winter horseshoes there that I'd never seen anywhere else, and also some rather primitive bleeding cups. I was also reminded that when a young Karelian couple got married they used to be expected to live together for the first winter in a tiny little hut with little warmth except themselves. I suppose it was one way of maintaining the level of the population . . .

Imatra races are world famous in the motorcycling world, but they are only part of Imatra week, held in July, in which there are carnivals, fêtes, exhibitions, etc., and which attracts something in the order of 160,000 people annually. I'm not sure where they put them all, but certainly one of the busiest places will be the Passiniemi camping site on the river bank. Wherever the visitors go, they will enjoy the informality of the town of Imatra. The people are easy-going and friendly, and I can't help feeling that a lot of this stems from the fact that they enjoy their freedom of thought and speech and movement, knowing only too well from experience and family what it is like without such things, for many of the citizens of Imatra are incomers from the lost lands. I was told that there is hardly a family in the town who didn't lose somebody between 1939/45 and that many lost everything when they turned their backs to the east. I have said elsewhere in this book that one of the most beautiful statues in Finland is 'Lament for Karelia' which stands in the war cemetery among the graves. I was not a little moved when I was told by a young local girl that when the students graduate they take flowers to the graves, both of the Winter War people and the Independence fighters. 'We owe them that,' she said.

I made one final visit in Imatra. This time to the Church of the Three Crosses, designed by Alvar Aalto. The three crosses are those of Christ and the robbers, and the church is designed in a flowing style which is repeated in every line, even on door handles and the ends of the chairs. It is beautiful, and extremely simple, and makes belief such an uncomplicated and easy process that one wonders why no-one had thought of it before.

It is 263 kilometres back to Helsinki from Imatra on the main road, but that means bypassing some of the most interesting parts of South Karelia and that is a pity—Lappeenranta for instance, which is the doorway to the Saimaa Canal at the southernmost end of Lake Saimaa, and which was founded by Queen Christina of Sweden in 1649. It has a rather interesting museum ship called *Princess Armada* in English, which has been turned into a café. It also possesses the Virgin Mary Church, the oldest Orthodox church in Finland; you can find it in the fortress, which itself was built in 1785. For those who are interested the largest inland war cemetery in Finland is in Lappeenranta.

But it is the canal which dominates the town for since its fifty kilometre length was reopened through territory leased from the U.S.S.R., Lappeenranta has become a terminal for traffic from Leningrad. The canal has eight huge locks which pass the ships downwards to the Gulf of Finland over a drop of over 200 feet, though one cannot see too much of this unless travelling by ship. These locks make all the little ones on Lake Saimaa look like toys, but they lack Saimaa's charm. For those of us who love the lakes and Karelia Lappeenranta is sufficient as journey's end.

However before returning from this enchanting land, let's visit Kotka, on the Gulf of Finland. It isn't really Karelia, but it still has a flavour of eastern Finland, so I have taken the liberty of including it in this chapter. I just hope the citizens won't mind and will take it as a compliment. One must go to Kotka to reach the islands of Kaunisaari and Hapasaari, two of the beloved holiday islands of the Gulf. They are only islands—wind, water, sunlight, rocks and little holiday houses— but they are an inseparable part of the atmosphere of summer Finland and you can arrange to stay with some of the fisherfolk.

Don't expect sophistication, but do expect the very winds of freedom; then you won't be disappointed.

Staying with a family in a holiday home is quite an experience. Accommodation is simple. The loos are usually dry, hung about with birch leaves to discourage midges, and about a day's march from the house, so one mustn't be in a hurry. The beaches may have a little sand, but more than likely they will consist of sun-warmed rocks so that you step cleanly from the water. And you are quite likely, if you are on a particularly quiet island, to meet a stark naked man coming from his swim after sauna. He will cover himself politely with one hand while carrying on a conversation to pass the time of day or the latest news, waving the other hand in the air betimes. You will eat the fish you have gone out to catch in the small boat of the family, and you will have brought all other requirements, including the beer, from the mainland. Washing presents no problem. There is always a sauna. As for clothes, who needs more than swimsuit, jeans and a sweater for the evenings? Try to ring a Finn after four in the summer in any town along the south coast or in the lake districts, and the answer is always the same. He's out on the islands. Don't fight it. Join him.

Kotka itself is a busy town whose wharves and ships bear witness to the immensity of the lumber industry in Finland. There aren't many tourist sights as such, mainly because the English destroyed the fortifications during the Crimean War. But there is one rather nice little place, and that is the fishing lodge given to Tsar Alexander II and his Danish wife, Dagmar. They loved the district and are given credit for founding Kotka as a town.

So, even here, the links with the east are strong. Not always welcome, but an inevitable part of past and present. The future? No-one has a crystal ball, but one can have hope as the Finns have, and make the most of enjoying what is, without doubt, one of the most poignant and evocative corners of today's Finland.

7. Helsinki and its Environs

When Tsar Alexander I moved the capital of his newly acquired Grand Duchy of Finland from Turku to Helsinki in 1812, it was mainly because he preferred to have the administration a little further away from its old master, Sweden, and nearer to his own capital of St Petersburg. He could never have realised what a service he was performing for generations of tourists yet to come, for by the very positioning of Helsinki near the mouth of the Vaantaa River so that one side of it was bounded by the sea, the city had to stay a compact one, and nearly all of Helsinki's most important buildings are within a comparatively small area. Growth has been enormous since that time, but it has been more in the nature of an extension to cope with the inevitable arrival of factories, housing and shipyards, so the essential flavour of Finland's capital is that of a small city—even, because of its marketplace by the harbour, a farmer's city by the sea, and one is always aware of the presence of natural things. Even the seagulls scream over the rooftops and drown the clatter of the trams . . .

Most of the main thoroughfares find their way to the water-side, even if changing names along the route, so it is not particularly difficult for a visitor to find his way around. The real problem comes when plunging into the residential streets, because Helsinki is the domain of flat dwellers and the grey blocks all look alike to the unpractised eye. The habit of putting the name of the street in Finnish and Swedish helps, but the signs are high on the wall, not easily seen from a small car. Like most cities, Helsinki is full of foreigners, for people want to see how the Finns have survived and prospered in spite of the hardships in the last thirty years. It is obvious that many like what they see, for one constantly meets 'settlers' despite the trying winter climate.

Tourist accommodation is more plentiful than it used to be. There are several new hotels, but it can still be difficult in mid-summer. There are also summer hotels, youth hostels and camping sites, and the schemes whereby one can get accommodation in a private house. This is very successful and far less expensive, though you might find, as I did, that communication between you and your hostess is hampered by lack of language, but there is a deal of smiling and pats on the back to reassure you that you are welcome. Hotels of course, speak a dozen tongues. I always enjoy staying at the old Seurahuone, purely because I love its atmosphere, its dark dining room with its tiny closed balconies, and its series of spacious landings with an assortment of heavy furnishings which must have been there in the days when it was the scene of many a brilliant social gathering under Tsarist rule.

The severe housing shortages which beset Helsinki after the last war, aggravated by the influx of refugees from lost Karelia, have been eased by the new housing areas which make their appearance some distance from the city. These are extremely pleasant. often set among tall trees on rocky ground which has been left in its natural state rather than confined into formal shapes, and the higher flats often command views over the heads of the forests, or towards the inlets of the Gulf. Most of these modern estates are well equipped with shopping facilities and each block always has its own sauna and storage rooms in the basement. But still one hears the complaint, 'It is such a long way into town.' One can understand this when remembering the effort it is to go out in midwinter, and the lack of daylight then. As in the rest of Scandinavia, people arrive early at work and leave early, so that they are able to use their leisure hours. This is particularly noticeable in summer, when the exodus from Helsinki is hair-raising as each driver becomes a Timo Makinnen along Mannerheimintie or Esplanadiskatu in his headlong escape to sauna, cottage or boat. Many citizens have summer houses on the islands of the archipelago or in the woods outside the city and when the summer school vacation begins entire families move there and father commutes. In winter they are all firmly entrenched in their snug, centrally heated apartments or houses, emerging to ski, to shoot off on a package tour to the Canaries, or to attend one of the many cultural activities such as ballet, opera, concerts, theatres, etc., which are always playing to capacity. Reading plays a large part in Finnish life, and apart from the excellent public libraries, bookshops, particularly Stockmanns, reputedly the largest in Western Europe, do big business all year.

There was probably a settlement at the mouth of the Vaantaa for centuries, but it was only in 1550 that King Gustavus Wasa of Sweden founded the town to compete as a trading post with Tallinn, on the other side of the Gulf. The wooden town was reduced to ashes in 1808, just at the time when Finland was changing masters, so the Tsar's move coincided with the necessity to rebuild the town. It could so easily have been just another northern city. Instead, the chairman of the reconstruction committee happened to be a far-sighted gentleman named Johan Albrecht Ehrenstrom, and he drew up the town plans between 1812 and 1815. The German-born architect Carl Ludwig Engel, was invited to Helsinki and he designed nearly all the buildings, including the Cathedral, which surround the Senate Square today, and which form what one might call the Whitehall of Helsinki. Apart from Olympic Tower, the steps of St Michael's Cathedral are an excellent vantage point if you can find a space, for they are usually occupied by young people, particularly at lunchtime in summer. From there you can see over the rooftops to the islands in the approaches of the harbour, the onions of the Uspenki Cathedral and the narrow streets which lead from Senate Square to Market Square, where the colourful striped awnings of the vendors lie between the Havis Amanda Statue and the obelisk marking the visit of Alexandra Federovna Tsarina of Russia.

The Senate Square is beautiful. A gem of design that any city would be proud to own. Spacious, gracious, a memory of a past

era, with a central statue of Tsar Alexander II who was popular
in Finland, it has been a silent witness to many of Finland's great
moments, a place where ordinary people have gathered at
turning points in Finnish history. It was here that workers
came in their flat caps and leather boots during the troubled era
that followed independence from Russia, attempting to take
over, as Lenin had taken over in the Smolny Palace in Petrograd;
it was here that the mourning crowds came to queue for the
long file past the mortal remains of Field-Marshal Mannerheim,
coming in their busloads from all over Finland to pay their
respects under the great dome of St Michael's; here that they
watched his last progress to Heitaniemi, carried by twelve
generals and followed by two thousand of his former officers,
many scarred from their service for Finland. It is still here that
people collect for the songs and hymns on Independence Day
each year on 6 December. At first glance, Senate Square looks
un-Finnish. On occasions such as these, it becomes the Finnish
heartbeat, and lives.

Mannerheimintie lives. It stretches down to join Esplanidis-
katu at the corner by the Swedish Theatre. A 'tall' road, like
its general, and along its length one finds the enormous bulk
of Stockmanns, several hotels and restaurants, some housed
in Sokos building, the Post Office, Parliament House, National
Museum, Helsinki City Museum, Finlandia Hall (first building
of the new city plan by Alvar Aalto) and much more. Parliament House can be visited, but if you are pressed for time nod
affably at the two gentlemen on statue guard near its door, Mr
Svinhufvud and Mr Stahlberg, both of whom played such huge
parts in the formation of Finland's present democratic way of
government, pause for a moment to look across the road at the
plinth where the Field-Marshal sits his famous horse Neptune,
a little apart, as he was in life, from the Parliament he helped to
found, and press on towards the National Museum.

This is another product of the national-Romantic type of
architecture so prevalent in Finland at the turn of the century.
Designed by Lindgren, Gesellius and Eliel Saarinen, it isn't a
beautiful building, yet it is interesting and imaginative and

does its job well. It traces Finland's life from prehistoric times to the present, leading one from one era to another in the most gentle and unobtrusive fashion but constantly matching the collection with its changing designs. Some of the most interesting items are found among the magnificent costumes from all over Finland because these show the influences at work through the centuries. The Lapland exhibits are exceptionally graphic and show many details of Lapp life. The musical collection shows the Finnish *kantele*, including one used by Elias Lönnrot, who in turn collected the *Kalevala*, and you can see fantastic illustrations from these stories in the frescoes, painted by Gallen-Kallela in the central hall. One of the most unique items is the triptych of the virgin St Barbara, brought from Kalanti Church. It was painted by a monk in a Dominican order in Hamburg, Master Francke, in the early fifteenth century and shows in idealised form how a young girl was tortured for her Faith and the eternal struggles between Good and Evil. No-one is sure how this work came to Kalanti, but tradition says it was found floating in the sea. Now it is a central piece in the church collection and must be priceless.

One comes bemused from this wealth of knowledge, past the small bear who guards the door, crosses the road and practically passes the elegant mansion set back from the road in formal gardens before realising that this is the Helsinki City Museum. If you are interested in getting a whiff of the city's atmosphere in the last century, this house is a must. It was built by Carl Johan Wallen, a Privy Councillor, in 1843 and was known then as Hagasalmi, or Villa Hagasund. It stood in beautiful estates and possessed many outbuildings. Some of these, together with a large part of the grounds, still exist. In 1860, the villa was inherited by Wallen's stepdaughter, Aurora Karamsin, and became the centre of many social activities of the Duchy, and must have been visited by all the great names, probably even the Russian royal family. In 1902 after Madame Karamsin died, first the land and then the house, came into the possession of the City of Helsinki and in 1912 it was opened as the City Museum. Some of the rooms have been kept as near as possible to Aurora's day, but others hold collections of arms, seals, portraits, etc. One of the most interesting is a copperplate engraving showing the building of Sveaborg fortress (Suomenlinna) and there is a watercolour by Carl Ludwig Engel, showing the Great Square. There is however, one exhibit about which I would like to tell you for it is a fascinating insight into everyday life of Helsinki, and it was because of this story that I had again tracked Mr Jarno Peltonen, the museum's Director, to earth in his over-crowded office at the villa.

On a Finnair flight from London to Helsinki I had been talking to a fellow passenger who had spent his childhood in the Munkeniemi district of Helsinki. In a flat above his parents' home there had dwelt an old man, who spoke little to his neighbours, except a courteous 'Good day'. The old chap had been taken ill and removed to the hospital, where he asked to see the caretaker of the apartment block. When the man arrived he told him that he knew he was dying, and that he had been a Russian engineer who had sought refuge in Helsinki after the Revolution; he asked the caretaker to go and search beneath a pile of clothes in his room and take a box he found to the Helsinki City Museum. (The caretaker said the room was completely poverty stricken and in chaos, but my informant did not see it himself.) The Russian, Mr Roussoff, said the box was 'my thank offering for my years in your city'. When the box was opened at the museum, it was found to contain several gold, silver and bejewelled eggs of the type which it had been fashionable for the wealthy of St Petersburg to give to friends at Easter, and on examination one was found to be by Fabergé, the master craftsman, and the rest by his pupils. They had lain in the room for about fifty years, and each one would have fetched enough money to have kept Mr Roussoff in comfort for his lifetime, but he preferred to pay his debt of freedom with them. 'Go and see them,' said my travelling companion. They *are* exquisite. Gold, enamel, set with mountain crystal, they are carefully displayed for all to see. Mr Peltonen said it was impossible to put an exact figure on them for they are collector's items.

I closed the iron gate of Villa Hagasund behind me, leaving the quiet gardens in the spring sunshine and coming back into the busy traffic of Mannerheimintie. Suddenly, Helsinki seemed, as it must have done so often to old Mr Roussoff, a very lovely place.

Almost next door to the Helsinki City Museum is Finlandia Hall, designed by Aalto, and opened at the end of December 1971. Acclaimed by many as the finest Concert Hall in Europe, it is a strangely shaped building, faced with white marble and picked out with glinting black granite. From Mannerheimintie it gives an impression of an opened grand piano, and from Tooloo Bay, which it faces, it reminds you of piano keys, but it is from inside that it is so very impressive. It is a symphony in black and white, delicately touched with copper and Finnish pine. It can be used for concerts, seating 1,750 people, and is the permanent home of the Helsinki City Orchestra. It has excellent restaurants and small rooms which can be hired for special functions, but most of all it has its eyes on the golden congress market, for few buildings in Scandinavia have its potential. The money is needed for it cost the city over £4,000,000 to build. It is worth taking a guided tour. You might even be lucky enough to be there, as I was, when the orchestra is rehearsing. Sibelius, of course.

The monument to Jean Sibelius stands in Sibelius Park, not far from the Children's Hospital and about half an hour's walk from the city centre. Designed by Eila Hiltunen, it is far more massive than one would think on first acquaintance for one can stand under the great steel pipes and get the feeling of walking into trees, or into a mighty organ. It shines and lives, and to me is one of the most beautiful things in Helsinki. Another beautiful thing is Taivallahti Church at Tempelliaukio, but like much of Finland it is not immediately obvious, and you can't just drive past to say 'I've seen it'. From outside there is a long low wall but on going through the glass doors one is within the living rock under a blazing dome of copper which brings out all the colours of the rock surfaces. One feels part of the elements within the church and the illusion is helped by clever use of daylight, particularly in the altar area. The designers, Timo and Tuomo Suomolainen, wanted their church to be warm, inviting, close to nature, and suitable to be used for concerts. That they succeeded is beyond doubt.

It is this combination of nature and art, sensitivity and practicality which is so typically Finnish and the natural things in Helsinki also include several islands which have their share of art and practicality in various forms. One of these islands is Seurasaari, reached by a footbridge from Meilahti. During summer this pleasant place with beaches, clear bathing water, restaurants and cafés is gay with folk dancing and concerts, because it also has a section of the National Museum in the form of old houses and a church which still functions in summer months. On Midsummer Evening one can see the church boats actually being used, while the great bonfire floats gently on the sea. Korkeasaari, another island, holds the city zoo, with many animals peculiar to the north, but it is Suomenlinna, or Sveaborg, that will be a focal point for history seekers, for the fortress, built across five islands, has been a chief player in the story of Finland, not always as hero.

The fortress was built during Swedish rule at the entrance to Helsinki Harbour, by Marshal Augustin Ehrensvard, whose picture hangs in the City Museum and whose grave is within Suomenlinna. The work was commenced in 1748 and the entire Finnish Army assisted in its building. It was remarkable for its time, and was considered impregnable, receiving the accolade 'Gibraltar of the North'. But it doesn't tower: it broods, a maze of tunnels and casemates. In 1808 however it surrendered to the Russians without a fight and after the Anglo-French bombardment in 1855 during the Crimean War, watched incidentally by the citizens of Helsinki from Observatory Hill, it was realised that under 'modern methods of warfare' it was outmoded. Now it is a romantic old place with towers, great walls and arches, and the wild flowers riot over the rusting cannon staring sightlessly at the sea. There are guided tours and museums, but locals go to enjoy the views or to visit the cafés and restaurants. The best of these is Walhalla, deep within the

thick walls near the Royal Gate, where the inscription roughly
translated reads 'Stand alone and trust no foreigners'. Boats to
Suomenlinna leave from South Harbour in summer only, and it
is a lovely trip on a fine day. There is a smaller, equally
attractive island in the Ehrensvard defences. This is Sarkän-
linna. It is not known to many tourists and is very much a
'local' haunt, but it has an attractive restaurant within the
thick walls of its castle too, where the floor is extremely sloping
and one dances uphill. The journey homeward towards
Helsinki on a summer night can be unforgettably beautiful.
Incidentally it is Sarkanlinna which is depicted in the background of Ehrensvard's portrait.

There are many restaurants in Helsinki, and it is impossible
to mention all of them, but two unusual ones are at Tervasaari
Island, reached by pontoon bridge and near the harbour
where many Helsinki people moor their boats, and where one
sees housewives still washing their rugs in the Baltic and drying
them on racks. Tervasaaren Aitta was formerly a tar store.
Pikinytky was once a tar boat which used to run on Lake
Saimaa. Both are fun, average but substantial food and not
madly expensive. In early morning get your coffee at the market
stall—it is the best in Helsinki.

Field-Marshal Mannerheim's home at Kalliolinnantie is now
a museum, full of little mementoes and trophies which were dear
to him and no visit to Finland is complete without paying him
some tribute, either there, or at his grave at Hietaniemi. The
cemetery is on a peninsula, so that the war graves are within
sight and sound of the waters of the Gulf, but it is not a sad
place, as Flanders is sad. The Field-Marshal's grave is starkly
simple. A massive grey stone engraved with one word: 'Mannerheim'. Again, it stands a little alone, yet surrounded by the
others who fought with him, and near to the great cross which
stands for them all. If you should be in Finland at Christmas
time, visit that cemetery on Christmas Eve. Lighted candles
are placed on each grave, and it is one of the most moving and
beautiful sights in the world.

There are so many more things to see in this old/new city.

The Olympic Stadium, built for the 1940 Games but unused until after the war, with its statue of Paavo Nurmi; the Art Museum in Ateneum opposite the impressive railway station built by Eliel Saarinen; the old National Theatre; the monument in the old town where the national anthem was sung for the first time; and many more. But find time to shop too, for this is a splendid place to spend money on worthwhile things. They won't be cheap, though. There are textiles, or dresses, by Marimekko, Rijy rugs, Bjorn Weckstrom jewellery in bronze, silver or gold, or the unique Kalevala Koru designs, delicate mobiles and fine candles from Arijekko, beautiful glassware and all Arabia's wares.

One could write a book on Arabia alone. Just over a hundred years ago, the Swedish firm of Rorstrand wanted to set up a subsidiary company in the then Grand Duchy in order to get a foothold in the Russian ceramic market. They found land which had belonged to a Finnish general who had called his villa 'Arabia', and his estate 'Land of Canaan', to remind him of his travels in the Near and Middle East. Arabia had to import white clay because there was none within Finland and with Finnish designers it began to produce items which caught the world's imagination. By 1916 Arabia had become independent from the parent Rorstrand and despite many ups and downs has never looked back. Now it is part of the giant Wärtsila shipbuilding concern and products include fine china, enamelware, earthenware, plastics and glassware, all of fine quality. You can visit the factories and their superb museum, but one place you are unlikely to see is the ninth floor at Vanhakaupunki, where, in twelve studios, some of the most famous names in Finnish art are at work. They are given complete freedom and unlimited raw materials; in return Arabia has a constant flow of ideas and motifs which often become bestsellers. Birger Kaipiainen, for example, has become renowned for his bead and mirror bird fantasies, but his designs for the mass market have resulted in the 'Paradise', 'Adam' and 'Eve' series put into production four years ago. Kai Franck worked for years in glass. His designs produced set after set of worldsellers, and now he is artistic director of Arabia and its sister Notsjö (Nuutajaarvi) Glass. Every studio is full of colour allied to genius. A few months later I was thrilled when I went on board one of the Royal Viking ships, built in Wärtsila yards, when she visited Southampton, and saw the very piece the designer had been working on during my visit.

Another 'real' place is Hvitträsk, about 18 miles from Helsinki and reached by road or by taking an electric train to Luoma and walking 2 kilometres. In 1902 three young architects, Gesellius, Lindgren and Saarinen, started to build a common studio and individual homes for themselves in one building. They were inspired by Gallen-Kallela's studio, and Hvitträsk's architecture and interior designs were to prove a cornerstone in Finnish design for generations to come The rooms follow the contours of the rocks on which the house is built: a few steps up, or down, a corridor, constantly changing sizes in doors and windows, a huge ceramic fireplace by Louis Sparr, a Rijy rug by Axel Gallen, embroidery by Eliel Saarinen's wife, Loja, ceramics by Finch. The house is crammed with items which cannot be seen anywhere else under one roof. There is a restaurant in an outhouse, and you can walk in the impressive grounds. All is part of the whole, as the three men intended. And again one is struck how far ahead of their time they all were.

I cannot honestly find the same enthusiasm for Dipoli, but then I don't pretend to understand it. It is quite fantastic, or splendid, depending on one's viewpoint. No two walls are alike. No window matches any other. No one material is a theme through the building. The only theme is nature. The ground floor for instance has a corridor which represents a river bed and even has rocks in it to heighten the effect. Built by Reima Pietila and Raili Paatelainen at Otaniemi, it is the students' activity centre, and certainly, the *teekkaris* of the Institute of Technology have a constant fillip to their own contributions to the future. It has a restaurant and in summer is a summer hotel, so you could stay there. Don't take *my* opinion: see for yourself!

It is not more than a few kilometres from Dipoli to Tapiola

Garden City, and you cannot remain indifferent to either of
them. Tapiola was the pioneer in Finnish town planning, a
remarkable example of teamwork between experts with con-
flicting ideas, for gardeners, welfare and social workers, heating
engineers, plumbers and planners, builders and electricians
pooled their resources to develop the designs of the twelve
architects into the place Tapiola is today. Completed in the
mid-1950s, gardens and parklands have matured now, towering
apartment blocks and small houses have a 'permanent' look,
and the ultramodern central area designed by Aarne Ervi is a
busy thriving place, still not outmoded by nearly twenty years
of living. Go up to the thirteenth floor of the tower and look out
from the restaurant. On a fine day they say you can see
Estonia. It comes as a surprise to people who have to commute
daily for journeys of one or more hours to learn that when
Tapiola was finally ready for habitation many people refused to
consider going there, because 'It was too long a journey', they
said. It is 9 kilometres from Helsinki. But now that the only
motorway in Finland runs close by, with a convenient turning-
off point, Tapiola has become one of the most sought-after
residential areas in the country. I know an Englishwoman who
lives there, and she wouldn't change her ultramodern flat with
its magnificent views of forest and skyscrapers for any other,
and I can't blame her.

I have deliberately left one excursion until last. From
Helsinki it is now possible to take a short visa-free cruise to the
u.s.s.r., visiting Leningrad or Tallin aboard the Finnish ship
Bore III. Many people, particularly from the United States,
choose this way of getting some idea of what life behind the
Iron Curtain can be like. I found it very worthwhile, and a
valuable opportunity of seeing some of the former palaces from
which Finland was once ruled.

8. Food, Drink and Sauna

'The Finns might not always be imaginative eaters, but by golly, they are sturdy ones.' That comment was made to me some years ago by an American I 'happened across'. We were both attacking the same cold table in a hotel in central Finland and had found ourselves side by side for about the fifth time on sorties to the central board and its goodies. The remark was accurate in some measure, because much of the wide variety offered today in so many excellent restaurants is due to foreign influence rather than coming from within the country, and the reasons can be found in history, geography and climate.

The main diet for many Finns is still based on grain, fats, meat and fish, with a marked lack of green vegetables, and medical opinion has inclined to say that this may account for the alarming incidence of heart disease. This has been noticed particularly in the district of north Karelia, where the rate of death due to heart conditions among men between 20 and 64 has been at something approaching 93 in every 10,000 and the high proportion has been put down to the fact that the fat content in the local diet is particularly high also. This is due no doubt to the fact that winters are fierce in northeastern Finland and to a long-held belief that fats keep up body warmth. This persists in spite of the modern way of living with central heating, deep-freezes, cars with heaters, etc., and so the habit of eating fats is deeply ingrained and not easily or quickly changed.

However, I have always found that if, within reason, one follows the customs of a country as far as food and drink are concerned one cannot go far wrong, for the people have evolved those customs, methods of cooking, flavouring and so forth to suit the way of life that they lead. Moreover it is highly unlikely that the holidaymaker or businessman visiting any country, and particularly such a clean one as Finland, would be adversely affected by so doing. One has to be living constantly in an environment for it to have any permanent influence on personal health, and there are so many interesting dishes to try out that it would be a pity to miss them.

There used to be a distinct division between the ways of cooking and eating in eastern and western Finland. This was mainly due to the existence of the great lakes of the central provinces which effectively barred communications and a free exchange of food and ideas; so in effect the eastern provinces eat in the way of Russia and the western in the way of Sweden, each adding their own flavour dependent on the foods found within their borders, and even now the distinction is there as one travels about Finland. For instance, within the great land masses of the east it was much more difficult to keep food fresh before the days of refrigeration, and therefore more salt was used in the preparation and cooking. In addition, people worked very long hours under terrible weather conditions, so the food was cooked inside the stove which kept the house warm and in a manner which would not spoil it if left for long periods. In the west the tendency was, and still is, towards more fish consumption, because it is readily available from the Baltic as well as from the lakes, and, because food was easier to obtain, the need for salt for preservation was not so high. In the north they had their own problems, most of which were solved by eating reindeer. Grain, particularly rye, was one crop which stood up to the vagaries of the climate and in the bad old days when there was frequent famine caused by the endless wars, destruction and crop failures, people got used to eating what was available. The same applies to root vegetables. The green ones were seldom seen, so one sees the pattern building over the centuries to the one used today.

Having said that, if I start off with the flat statement that 'Finns have a predilection for sausages' it would provide a heaven sent opportunity for anyone not really interested in trying out Finnish specialities to skip the rest of the chapter on the assumption that all I am going to write about is sausages, beer and sauna, for the three are almost inseparable. But I must devote just a little space to the *makkara* as the Finns call sausage, because it is very definitely part of the way of life there, lending itself to being eaten as an open sandwich, cooked on the sauna stove or on campfires, or on the more sophisticated barbecueing equipment found at cottages or on boats during the great Finnish exodus to the outdoor life. Makkara comes in a variety of flavours, many of them very similar to the Continental varieties which have crept into foodstores in the u.k. in recent years, with no resemblance at all to the 'British banger'. I have it from very reliable sources that makkara forms half of the approximately 46 kilos of meat consumed *per capita* each year in Finland. But there are two specialities which must be given special mention. These are the *poromakkara* and the *saunamakkara* called *linkki*. *Poro* means reindeer and therefore poromakkara means a sausage made from reindeer meat. These are rather dark in colour, extremely tasty and rather expensive, for reindeer is as much of a delicacy today as bear meat. The linkki is similar to, but somewhat thicker than a frankfurter, and with a special smoky salty flavour. I always suspect that the smoky taste is put there so that it doesn't matter if you drop the sausage in the fire a few times, and the salt ensures that if you haven't developed a thirst in the sauna, the makkara soon remedies that. Makkara wouldn't taste right without one of the many varieties of bread, which is eaten in enormous quantities, for the reasons already outlined. There is a tremendous selection, mostly dark breads, but nowadays there seems to be an increase in the number of white breads available. I find the latter haven't the flavour of, say, French white bread, or even of the British plastic loaf, and I am inclined to stick to the superb rye and black breads offered on every table, along with the flat and crispbreads so universally popular. Of these too, there are special ones, and my own favourite is the one sprinkled with poppy seeds.

Rye is used much more than oats for porridge, either rolled or as meal, and the resultant dish is darker and coarser in texture with a nutty flavour. It is served with butter, milk and sugar, is very filling, and makes a fine start to a dark snowy morning.

Coffee is usually very good. Finns are a nation of coffee drinkers and get through enormous quantities, something like twenty pounds per person per year. Milk too can be said to be a national beverage and the consumption is about five hundred pints per person per year. I think this figure includes the various derivatives like buttermilk, low fat milk, yoghourt, etc., and the delightful *viili* curd, served with cinnamon and sugar, but even so this is a very high figure by any standards. Perhaps this compensates for their inherent inability to make tea, but one cannot have everything, and one can always run away to a Russian restaurant in Helsinki and find the marvellous tea served with spoonfuls of raspberry jam!

Any main meal served without potatoes is unthinkable, and invariably, as in the rest of Scandinavia, they come plain boiled, perhaps with butter and parsley or dill, or more than likely with brown sauce. They are particularly precious to the Finn in late spring and early summer when the new crop arrives in Helsinki market place and one sees stallkeepers selling nothing else but the small golden treasures. Treasures is the right word. I was having dinner with friends this summer and the husband had done the shopping. It was with glee that he confided to me that he had splashed out on new potatoes for a special treat. 'Two marks each potato,' he said. 'But you don't come every day. It is worth it.' I felt humbled, and yet honoured . . .Potatoes are so much part of the Finnish scene that it comes as somewhat of a surprise to find that when the potato was introduced by soldiers returning from the German wars about three hundred years ago, it was disliked and refused in favour of the turnip already used in Scandinavia for centuries as a staple food. It wasn't until the Finns found out about a hundred years later that potatoes could make excellent spirits that it finally found favour, and nowadays it plays a very large role in the diet of Finland, both in its edible form as well as its liquid one.

When most of Karelia was annexed by Russia at the end of the Second World War, many Karelians moved into other parts of Finland taking their own cultures and traditions with them, and in consequence a number of Karelian dishes have found their way on to everyday menus. Root vegetables form many of the main ingredients, and one dish holds pride of place in the popularity stakes. It is is called *Lanttulaatikko*, and is made from turnips. These are boiled and sieved, added to breadcrumbs, butter, eggs, cream, salt and nutmeg (you will see that all these ingredients would have been readily available in the farmlands of the east, even the nutmeg, which would have come across the landmass with the spice trains). It is all placed in a casserole and baked slowly. It sounds horrible, but I can assure you it is delicious, and there is a similar dish made from carrots, called *Porrkanalaatikko*. Another favourite is Karelian Hot-Pot, prepared from mutton, pork and veal, all cooked together with salt, pepper and onions for hours on end, and again, served with boiled potatoes and turnips. Its Finnish name is *Karjalanpaisti*, and for the benefit of those who like to try out the odd dish or two, I am including the recipe at the end of this section (p. 210). There is also a special pasty from Karelia, called *Keitinpiirakka*, stuffed with cooked whole dry rice and served with a mixture of hardboiled eggs and butter, and there is *sultsina*, a very thin pancake filled with a sweetened thick rice pudding (this last is not a dish which is found everywhere. I have only tasted it once, in Karelia, and I still remember it with some nostalgia).

There are meatballs of course, though the Finnish propensity for these is reflected all over Scandinavia, as any visitor to these countries (or to the Canary Islands, winter stronghold of the Northerners) will know! There are the more exotic things, whose origins are Russian, like Bortsch—made from beetroot and vegetable soup and served with sour cream—or blinis, a buckwheat pancake eaten with caviare, chopped onions and sour cream, and there are the famous pasties from Kuopio called *Kallakukko*, in which the fish and pork are baked together inside the rye bread or pastry. This last dish is a purely Finnish invention, and comes directly from the days when the men worked long hours in the forests, or on the islands in the lakes, and had to carry food with them. It was easier to carry the fillings inside the covering, and that too, came from the days when bread was scarce or non-existent, for there have been many of those in the past. For instance, at one time at the beginning of the eighteenth century food was so scarce that people made bread from the bark of trees—with extremely adverse results. At Kompero, not far from Joenssu in Karelia, I was shown the type of mortar bowl in which the bark was pounded for use, and the caretaker of the old cottage made a great play of a pantomime of stomach ache . . . No wonder.

In the far north there was generally a good supply of reindeer for the use of the locals and it was on the menu even in bad years. The Lapps existed on it in every form—dried, smoked, fresh and salted in stews or in chewing strips, like the biltong of Africa. The lack of fresh vegetables in their diet resulted in the severe rickets that one sees still in old people in the area. There was also the occasional bear killed, although this was in some measure a ritual which would bring good luck. The luck was probably the meat, which supplied the community for days. Rivers provided salmon, and until the end of the nineteenth century this was considered to be a basic food. It was so common-place that there was a ruling that salmon could only be fed to servants once a week! Nowadays, all these three foodstuffs, once primary, are extremely expensive delicacies. For example a small piece of smoked reindeer will cost upwards of £3. Even more costly are reindeers' tongues, which are served in restaurants with lemon sauce and cranberries to bring out the delicate flavour. The first time I tasted them is very clear in my mind, for it was a highlight in my Finnish saga. I'd been invited to dine at Kalastajatorrpa, the famous 'Fisherman's Cottage' in Helsinki, by Finnish friends. It was summer; the weather was, as it so often is in June, splendid, and we sat by the long windows on the second floor, looking out over the trees by the lakeside, while my hosts introduced me to a succession of Finnish specialities. *Graavilohi*, a specially prepared and marinated salmon, reindeer tongues, *suomurainen*, the special Arctic berries, surmounted by cream, and Finnish liqueurs and wines. I've never forgotten it. And I must admit that ever since I have felt slightly guilty at what it must have cost them to do that. But that is the measure of Finnish hospitality. One can only say 'thank you' and mean it from the heart.

There is an abundance of fish to choose from. Particularly good are the sprats and herrings from the Baltic. There is one excellent dish, made from fresh herring, called Shoemakers' Salmon, popular in the northwest. In addition herring salads are legion, but these involve a rich dressing which is kin to the Swedish ones used just across the sea. There are so many ways of serving herring and while they are still basically 'herring flavour' they are all subtly and delicately different. Then there are the lampreys. These are small eels which are delicious, but which might be considered an acquired taste. There are the whitefish or *sik*, cousin to trout. There are *muikko*—vendace as we know them, which come from the Lake Saimaa region and are kin to sardines, but smaller still. And of course there are the two royal dishes: crayfish—those elegant, succulent creatures that are only caught in July or August and supply the main excuse for many a summer party; one has to wear a bib to eat them in the 'proper' manner, but, once eaten under a summer Scandinavian sky, they too are never forgotten—and salmon itself, served grilled, or marinated, as I have said, or boiled, and usually served with a mushroom sauce. The best mushroom sauce that I have ever tasted was made at the Rantasipi hotel at Hyvinkaa from *Korvasigni*, a rather special wild mushroom, and incidentally, it is to the chef at this hotel that I am also indebted for the cauliflower soup recipe which also appears in this book. It is one of the most delicious soups that one can find anywhere, but it is not for weightwatchers!

But there is one dish to which I can never become addicted. This is dried cod. It is called *lootfisk* in Norway, but I have never found out its Finnish name, or to be more accurate, I have never wanted to! It has to be preserved for some time, and tastes like it. I remember one terrible evening when it was served to me as a special treat at a private houseparty, and in order not to offend, I ate it as quickly as possible, washing it down with a beer. Imagine my horror when I was immediately plied with more by my delighted hostess, who was convinced that she had chosen exactly the right thing to please me. How could I disillusion her? Not at all. So I ate it all again, but much more slowly. . .

I have never been particularly fond of soup either, with the exception of the Rantasipi one mentioned above, but the ones so often served as the main dish in Finnish homes are enough to change my tastes. Fish is often used, so too are meat and vegetables, and of the latter there is one particular soup which should be mentioned. It is made from green peas, is called *hernekietto*, and traditionally eaten on Thursdays. I have yet to discover why. One which only makes its appearance in summer is *kesakeitto* (summer soup, what else?) and is made from very young vegetables. It is light, very pleasant and very easy to make. There are also several cheese soups, but I prefer cheese in its 'raw' state. The familiar 'loaf' cheese puts in a regular appearance on Finnish breakfast tables, though one also gets a lot of processed cheeses in those irritating little silver wrappers these days. But there are other excellent cheeses, particularly the one made in Turku. This doesn't keep, so it can only be eaten in the place of origin to taste it to perfection. In restaurants, except in deep country districts, you have to ask for local cheese if you want to try it, or you will get the standard cheeses we can now buy in the U.K. They are good but unexciting.

Apart from the abominable lootfisk, which is reputedly a Christmas delicacy, there is another Christmas dish called *riisipuro*. This is a kind of unsweetened rice pudding in which an almond is hidden, much in the way that we used to conceal silver threepenny bits in our Christmas puddings. The one who gets the almond is supposed to marry within the year, so mother has to be careful who gets what helping! But in any case, the recipient is supposed to have good luck, so all is well. To compensate the almondless or the lootfiskhaters, the next dish at Christmas is usually Christmas ham (*joulukinkko*), which is specially cured. I suppose it is one stage on from the pork eaten elsewhere in Scandinavia, or our own pork and goose traditions.

No mention of Finnish food would be complete without some comment upon the cold table, which is so very popular with foreign visitors. This is an import into Finland from the rest of Scandinavia, and anyone who is at all familiar with the finer aspects of a cold table can tell at once whether he is in Norway, Sweden, Denmark or Finland, for each differs slightly, not only in the dishes served, but in the methods of preparation and presentation. For instance the Finnish table is not nearly so reliant on mayonnaises as the Swedish one, which may be because the Finns seem to prefer the natural flavours of food. The emphasis is usually on the cold fish and meat, but there are always a number of hot dishes to be found on the hot plates at the end of the table. When it comes to sweets, Finnish tastes usually lie towards rich gâteaux, often served with coffee in the afternoon, rather than with the lunch-time cold table, but the cheeses are usually there in super-abundance. By the way, the name for the cold table is *voileipä-poyta*, if you are looking for it on a menu, and there are always excellent ones at the top Helsinki Hotels, at Hesperia, at Bankett Hilden, at Hamburger Bors in Turku, Rantasipi at Hyvinkaa and elsewhere, and on the ferries to and from Finland from everywhere.

Fruit is not a feature of the menus, and I for one do miss it and often end up in the marketplaces of the towns to buy my own supplies (no more expensive than in Britain in summer time). But there is one big compensation in the form of the fresh or frozen berries, such as strawberries, blueberries, raspberries or cranberries, or the famous and aforementioned suomurainen ('cloudberries' in English, though they don't grow in the U.K., *multer* in Norwegian, and *hjørtron* in Swedish), served with whipped cream and/or pancakes, and my resistance to these is nil. I never feel I have been to Scandinavia unless I have had one of these at least once during my stay. The cream is fatal to the waistline, but the sauna can take care of that, one hopes. . .

You can get good beers and wines and spirits, served in restaurants and in *grillibaari*, but it is a very expensive business and it is more than you dare do to have a drink and drive after it. That is quite sufficient to put you in jail without the option for six months, and being a foreigner just won't be good enough to let you off. On meeting friends for dinner, take a taxi. The mere suggestion that one takes a car is met with such horror and cries of 'that would spoil the party, because then you cannot drink' so I gave up after the first few attempts. Mind you, the law is justified. Alcoholism is still a very real problem and one does see drunks in the streets in every city, not just in Helsinki. People seem to disregard them entirely, virtually stepping over or round them, but I have also seen a policeman trying to encourage a *juoppo* to go home, without much success. Surprisingly, the policeman shrugged and walked away, which is apparently the normal reaction.

People accept that there is a problem. It has been blamed on many things: weather, temperament, history, the lean years, but it is I think a combination of them all, and it is by no means a new difficulty. It goes back for hundreds of years, for like many other country folk, Finns have made their own beer and spirits for generations from all sorts of things. The first wines made their way to Finland somewhere about the Middle Ages, but the problem of drinking grew gradually. Even about three hundred years ago the government in Turku, then the capital, issued instructions on who could drink what and when, at festive occasions like weddings. They said that while a mayor could offer his guests as much as he could afford, with no restrictions, the craftsman and artisan could only have French wine and Finnish beer. Not much notice was taken of this, as you might imagine, and after the introduction of the ubiquitous potato there was a veritable flood of illicit stills up and down the land, brewing *pontikka*, as the liquor is called, with inevitable results. It was probably not too dangerous to anyone except the drinker himself while the days of horsedrawn traffic still existed, for the sagacious animal could be relied upon to take his master safely home, but the motor can perform no such service. Finally there were so many deaths and injuries not only from drunken driving but from the effects of alcoholic poisoning that the law cracked down, the stills were outlawed and the drinking of pontikka forbidden. This happened all over Scandinavia for the problems didn't only apply to Finns. Swedes, Norwegians, Icelanders and Danes were equally culpable, and their reputation as hard drinkers, or at least as drinkers with hard heads, when they emigrated to other lands was to a very great extent justified. Perhaps this does throw some light on the reason why alcohol is still so much under government control and why each country has such stringent licensing rules.

ALKO is the official Finnish Government Agency, constantly vetting the content and standard of official drinks and imports, issuing licences to restaurants, breweries, etc., bottling large imports of wines and running the official alcohol stores. It is one of the sights of Finland for a foreigner to see queues of solemn Finnish gentlemen, all with their briefcases, waiting to replenish the house supplies, usually on a Friday afternoon. In other countries briefcases are presumed to contain pyjamas, but in Finland they are guaranteed to produce a bottle or two on the day before a public holiday. There has been some slight relaxation of the law in so far as one can purchase light beer from a grocery store, but all else comes under the auspices of ALKO and it is very expensive. You don't get much change from seven pounds for a bottle of whisky, so don't forget to take your duty frees from the ship or aircraft. If you don't drink yourself, it is ten to one your hosts will and will be delighted with your contribution to their drinks cupboard. Not that it will stay there very long!

Finnish wines and liqueurs were completely unknown outside Finland until recently, but the liqueurs, along with many other Finnish products, are finding a lot of favour overseas. When lunching at Koli one day I tried a dry white wine called Elysee. It was a Moussec type, made by Marli, and was pleasant enough to drink, but no wine by French or German standards. But it is worth trying them; after all, who expects wines to be made in Finland? There are at present five firms making wines and liqueurs and among the best known of these are Lignell and Piispanen, of Kuopio, and Marli of Turku. Both these firms make excellent liqueurs from the wild berries of the countryside. For instance there is Lacca, made from the cloudberry found in northern and central Finland. The berry is apricot in colour and resembles a blackberry in shape, although its leaf is more like that of a strawberry. It grows in the swamps and marshes and has become scarce, so that a considerable amount of effort is now being expended to cultivate it under natural conditions, for it could bring considerable revenue to poorer regions. Another liqueur is Mesimarja, made from the tiny arctic bramble, and much more difficult to obtain, even within Finland. This is exceedingly sweet, but very delicately flavoured. Then, there is Polar, with the tart fresh flavour of cranberries. This is good served with ice.

Vodka—*koskenkorva*—is widely consumed all over Finland. There are various types, all equally potent, and a few glasses of these are guaranteed to cause no pain until morning. Schnapps or aquavit, is the inevitable accompaniment to a cold table, washed down with one of the light Finnish beers. Lahden Export is pleasant and there are other local brews, but don't be tempted into drinking the *low* percentage beer found in roadside cafés and supermarkets—it is rather like soapsuds. No mention of drinks would be complete without *Glögg*, made from aquavit, vermouth, red wine, spices and dried fruits; it is delicious. Don't let the fruit fool you. Several of these in quick succession and no-one is fit to drive from any party anywhere!

RECIPES

Karelian Hotpot

Place equal portions of mutton, pork and veal cut in pieces about an inch square in an earthenware dish. Add water so that half of the meat is covered and put the dish into the oven. Brown for about an hour, add salt and allspice to taste. Cover with lid and cook in the oven for about six hours, adding water if necessary. Serve with boiled potatoes and stewed turnips.

Rantasipi Cauliflower Soup (serves 6)

For the stock:
  1 carrot
  ¼ onion
  ¼ leek
  1 parsnip
  stalks of 1 cauliflower
  black and white peppercorns to taste
  2 oz butter

For the rest:
  1 heaped tablespoon flour
  1 oz butter
  1 pt veal stock
  1 pt thin cream
  buds from 1 cauliflower
  salt
  ground white pepper

Method: Cut stock ingredients into smallish pieces and cook in the butter over a low heat for about 15 minutes. Melt the other butter, add flour and cook for 15 minutes. Add veal stock and cream, both gently warmed, and stock and cook all ingredients together for 20 minutes. Strain into another saucepan, add pre-cooked cauliflower buds and flavour with salt and ground white pepper. If soup is too thick add cauliflower stock. Take care to avoid lumps.

Glögg

  2 bottles vodka or aquavit
  2 bottles dry vermouth
  2 bottles dry red wine
  5 prunes, 10 dried apple rings, 3 dried peaches, 1 dried pear, 4 dried apricots
  5 dried orange peels
  3 sticks cinnamon

2 tablespoons cloves
1 cup raisins
10 almonds
20 cardamon seeds (whole)
1 small ginger root
1 cup sugar

Method: Soak spices in 5 cups of water for 4 hours. Add 1 cup sugar and boil slowly for 15–25 minutes. Remove cinnamon sticks and let all spices cool in water. Drain and squeeze out water. Mix with spirits and wine, heat and serve in cups with 2 teaspoons of raisins and 2 almonds. Enough for 30 happy people!

Sauna. . . No book on Finland would be complete without reference to it, for it is inseparable from the way of life. It is almost another religion. Finns use the sauna not only as a physical cleansing but almost as a recharging of spiritual batteries. I've seen a faraway look in a Finn's eyes in London when talking of going home to his summer cottage, where, he said, 'The sauna will be waiting.' I've been met at Helsinki airport by friends who have ushered me into a taxi saying, 'Hurry, we have a sauna booked,' and I've been driven miles across Lapland, placed in a small motorboat and hurtled towards an island over a lake crackling with newly formed ice just so that I could sample the family's prize possession, a smoke sauna (and jump in the lake afterwards . . .). Asking someone to come for sauna is one of the greatest compliments that can be bestowed. It is NOT AT ALL the same as offering the use of a bathroom!

Sauna has been used in Finland for two thousand years and originally was a burrow in the earth where stones (*klua*) were heated and water thrown on them to produce steam, called *löyly*. The sweating process was and still is often helped along by using a bunch of leaves tapped on the skin. Sauna was always a central point in the home. Women were taken there for confinement, a sensible process, for it is clean, has plenty of hot

water, and one relaxes there. Brides were always given sauna
before going to the altar, and old people were often taken there
in their last hours. After the devastation of war, sauna was
always the first thing to be rebuilt, for people could live in that
building, certain of heat and hot water, while the rest of the
living quarters were reconstructed. It was also used as a drying
place for flax or a curing store for meat. But it also had its roots
in superstitions; the age-old beliefs in every land in the proper-
ties of fire and the need for purification are very deep. There
used always to be three shifts for the sauna: one for men, one for
women, and one for the sauna sprites. No human would ever
use the third shift . . .

Nowadays the sauna cult is spreading throughout the world,
but there is still something special in taking one in Finland,
particularly beside a Finnish lake, where one jumps into clear
unpolluted water, or rolls in the snow. I'm no Spartan, and
normally cannot be inveigled into cold water of any kind, but
honestly one doesn't feel the cold after sauna and the feeling of
well-being is unbelievable. Finnish businessmen often take their
visitors to sauna as it is private, so confidential things can be
discussed, and hostility or suspicion is often shed with the
clothes. It is hard to remain unfriendly sitting on the cool wood
of the spruce platforms clad only in one's birthday suit.

There are special shops in Helsinki supplying everything for
sauna use, but the impedimenta can also be found in iron-
mongers' or big department stores and many of these items can
be bought in the u.k. imported direct from Finland, no more
expensively. Not everyone uses the *vihta* or whisk, made from
twigs of young birch leaves, but I must say I find it very
pleasant. It is a gentle movement and the leaves give the skin
a fresh scent. It is NOT a masochistic action, rather the reverse.
In public saunas there is always a bath attendant, usually
female and elderly, who will scrub you if you wish. This is pure
luxury, and there is no embarrassment on either side.

One emerges from the experience to relax in the adjoining rest
room and thoroughly cool off, and perhaps, to eat a makkara,
cooked on the rest room fire, *never* on the kluas, and drink a beer.

Dressing too quickly can be uncomfortable. One cannot hurry sauna, any more than one can hurry Finland.

It is not until one has taken sauna in Finland, preferably at someone's home, that one can understand a little better how a Finn looks at life. I remember one occasion, when the new leaves on a birch tree appeared in a garden where patchy snow still lay on the ground, and my host spotted them. 'Good,' he exclaimed. 'Soon we can make the new *vihta*.' To him the rebirth of spring brought the pleasures not only of nature, but of sauna too. The two are indivisible.

Index